Lecture Notes in Computer Science   15429

Founding Editors

Gerhard Goos
Juris Hartmanis

Chunxiao Xing · Jiacai Lai · Liang-Jie Zhang
Editors

Metaverse – METAVERSE 2024

20th International Conference
Held as Part of the Services Conference Federation, SCF 2024
Bangkok, Thailand, November 16–19, 2024
Proceedings

 Springer

Editors
Chunxiao Xing 🆔
Tsinghua University
Beijing, China

Liang-Jie Zhang 🆔
Shenzhen University
Shenzhen, China

Jiacai Lai 🆔
Lecheng Times Technology Co., Ltd
Beijing, China

ISSN 0302-9743 ISSN 1611-3349 (electronic)
Lecture Notes in Computer Science
ISBN 978-3-031-76976-4 ISBN 978-3-031-76977-1 (eBook)
https://doi.org/10.1007/978-3-031-76977-1

This Springer imprint is published by the registered company Springer Nature Switzerland AG
The registered company address is: Gewerbestrasse 11, 6330 Cham, Switzerland

If disposing of this product, please recycle the paper.

Preface

To rapidly respond to the changing economy, the World Congress on Services has been naturally extended to become the International Conference on Metaverse to cover immersive services for all vertical industries and area solutions. With the emergence of Metaverse, the current services will be gradually transformed into immersive services that construct digital worlds and connect with physical worlds. The immersive services are the core characteristics of Metaverse.

METAVERSE 2024 was a member of the Services Conference Federation (SCF). SCF 2024 had the following 10 collocated service-oriented sister conferences: 2024 International Conference on Web Services (ICWS 2024), 2024 International Conference on Cloud Computing (CLOUD 2024), 2024 International Conference on Services Computing (SCC 2024), 2024 International Conference on Big Data (BigData 2024), 2024 International Conference on AI & Multimodal Services (AIMS 2024), 2024 International Conference on Metaverse (METAVERSE 2024), 2024 International Conference on Internet of Things (ICIOT 2024), 2024 International Conference on Cognitive Computing (ICCC 2024), 2024 International Conference on Edge Computing (EDGE 2024), and 2024 International Conference on Blockchain (ICBC 2024).

This volume presents the accepted papers of the 2024 International Conference on Metaverse (METAVERSE 2024), held in Bangkok, Thailand during November 16–19, 2024. For this conference, each paper was single-blind reviewed by three independent members of the International Program Committee. After carefully evaluating their originality and quality, we have accepted 10 papers.

We are pleased to thank the authors whose submissions and participation made this conference possible. We also want to express our thanks to the Organizing Committee and Program Committee members, for their dedication in helping to organize the conference and reviewing the submissions. We owe special thanks to the keynote speakers for their impressive speeches.

Finally, we would like to thank operations team members Jing Zeng, Sheng He, Yishuang Ning, and Zhuolin Mei for their excellent work in organizing this conference. We look forward to your future great contributions as a volunteer, author, and conference participant in the fast-growing worldwide services innovations community.

September 2024

Chunxiao Xing
Jiacai Lai
Liang-Jie Zhang

Organization

General Chair

Shiping Chen   CSIRO Data61 & UNSW, Australia

Program Chair

Chunxiao Xing   Tsinghua University, China

Application Track Chair

Jiacai Lai   Lecheng Times Techonology Co., Ltd., China

Services Conference Federation (SCF 2024)

General Chairs

Ali Arsanjani   Google, USA
Wu Chou   Essenlix Corporation, USA

Coordinating Program Chair

Liang-Jie Zhang   Shenzhen University, China

CFO and International Affairs Chair

Min Luo   Georgia Tech, USA

Operation Committee

Jing Zeng	China Gridcom Co., Ltd., China
Yishuang Ning	Tsinghua University, China
Sheng He	Kingdee International Software Group Co., Ltd., China
Zhuolin Mei	Jiujiang University, China

Steering Committee

Calton Pu (Co-Chair)	Georgia Tech, USA
Liang-Jie Zhang (Co-Chair)	Shenzhen University, China

METAVERSE 2024 Program Committee

Xinxin Fan	IoTeX, USA
Xiaohu Fan	Wuhan Collage, China
Hongyu Tian	Chinese Academy of Sciences, China
Kunjing Zhang	Institute of Information and Technology, China
Ben Falchuk	Peraton Labs, USA
Xiuhua Li	Chongqing University, China
Waseem Akhtar Mufti	Freelancer, Pakistan
Shigeng Zhang	Central South University, China

Conference Sponsor – Services Society

The Services Society (S2) is a non-profit professional organization that has been created to promote worldwide research and technical collaboration in services innovations among academia and industrial professionals. Its members are volunteers from industry and academia with common interests. S2 is registered in the USA as a "501(c) organization", which means that it is an American tax-exempt nonprofit organization. S2 collaborates with other professional organizations to sponsor or co-sponsor conferences and to promote an effective services curriculum in colleges and universities. S2 initiates and promotes a "Services University" program worldwide to bridge the gap between industrial needs and university instruction.

The Services Sector accounted for 79.5% of the GDP of the USA in 2016. The Services Society has formed 5 Special Interest Groups (SIGs) to support technology- and domain-specific professional activities.

- Special Interest Group on Services Computing (SIG-SC)
- Special Interest Group on Big Data (SIG-BD)
- Special Interest Group on Cloud Computing (SIG-CLOUD)
- Special Interest Group on Artificial Intelligence (SIG-AI)
- Special Interest Group on Metaverse (SIG-Metaverse)

About the Services Conference Federation (SCF)

As the founding member of the Services Conference Federation (SCF), the first **International Conference on Web Services (ICWS)** was held in June 2003 in Las Vegas, USA. Meanwhile, the First International Conference on Web Services - Europe 2003 (ICWS-Europe 2003) was held in Germany in October 2003. ICWS-Europe 2003 was an extended event of the 2003 International Conference on Web Services (ICWS 2003) in Europe. In 2004, ICWS-Europe was changed to the European Conference on Web Services (ECOWS), which was held at Erfurt, Germany. Sponsored by the Services Society and Springer, SCF 2018 and SCF 2019 were held successfully in Seattle and San Diego, USA. SCF 2020 and SCF 2021 were held successfully online and in Shenzhen, China. SCF 2022 and 2023 were held successfully in Hawaii, USA. To celebrate its 21st birthday, SCF 2024 was held on November 16–19, 2024, in Bangkok, Thailand.

In the past 21 years, the ICWS community has expanded from Web engineering innovations to scientific research for the whole services industry. Service delivery platforms have been expanded to mobile platforms, Internet of Things, cloud computing, and edge computing. The services ecosystem has gradually been enabled, value added, and intelligence embedded through enabling technologies such as big data, artificial intelligence, and cognitive computing. In the coming years, all transactions with multiple parties involved will be transformed to blockchain.

Based on technology trends and best practices in the field, the Services Conference Federation (SCF) will continue serving as the conference umbrella's code name for all services-related conferences. SCF 2024 defined the future of New ABCDE (AI, Blockchain, Cloud, BigData & IOT) and entered the 5G for Services Era. The theme of ICWS 2024 was Web-based Services for Metaverse Era. We are very proud to announce that SCF 2024's 10 co-located theme topic conferences all centered around "services", with each focusing on exploring different themes (web-based services, cloud-based services, Big Data-based services, services innovation lifecycle, AI-driven ubiquitous services, blockchain-driven trust service ecosystems, industry-specific services and applications, and emerging service-oriented technologies).

- Bigger Platform: The 10 collocated conferences (SCF 2024) were sponsored by the Services Society, which is the world-leading not-for-profit organization (501(c)(3)) dedicated to the service of more than 30,000 worldwide Services Computing researchers and practitioners. A bigger platform means bigger opportunities for all volunteers, authors, and participants. Meanwhile, Springer provided sponsorship of the best paper awards and other professional activities. All the 10 conference proceedings of SCF 2024 were published by Springer and indexed in the ISI Conference Proceedings Citation Index (included in Web of Science), Engineering Index EI (Compendex and Inspec databases), DBLP, Google Scholar, IO-Port, MathSciNet, Scopus, and ZBlMath.
- Brighter Future: While celebrating the 2024 version of ICWS, SCF 2024 highlighted the International Conference on AI and Multimodal Services (AIMS 2024) to build

the fundamental infrastructure for enabling AIGC services ecosystems. It will also lead our community members to create their own brighter future.

– Better Model: SCF 2024 continued to leverage the invented Conference Blockchain Model (CBM) to innovate the organizing practices for all the 10 theme conferences. Senior researchers in the field are welcome to submit proposals to serve as CBM Ambassador for an individual conference to start better interactions during your leadership role in organizing future SCF conferences.

Contents

Research Track

OCCL-Former: Data Augmentation Driven Occlusion-Aware Inter-Body Parts Relationship Learning for 3D Pose Estimation

Md. Imtiaz Hossain[1], Sharmen Akhter[1], Sungjun Yang[2], and Eui-Nam Huh[1(✉)]

[1] Computer Science and Engineering, Kyung Hee University, Giheung-gu, Yongin-si, Gyeonggi-do 17104, Republic of Korea
{hossain.imtiaz,sharmen,johnhuh}@khu.ac.kr
[2] SIGONGtech, Seongnam-si, Republic of Korea
yangsj@sigongtech.co.kr

Abstract. Though existing 3D human pose estimation approaches achieve significant performance improvements, they struggle under occlusions. To mitigate this challenge, we propose OCCL-Former, a novel Trans**Former**-based **OCCL**usion method that implicitly learns the dependencies and relationships among body parts to accurately infer occluded body regions exploiting visible information. Firstly, OCCL-Former estimates the interrelationships between body parts and joints during training using augmented inputs. By leveraging augmented data to extract global contextual information and dependencies, OCCL-Former robustly handles occlusions. During training, we simulate occlusions by introducing noise to obscure specific body parts while providing full-body visuals as targets, thereby enabling the model to learn comprehensive inter-joint dependencies. The proposed architecture employs two transformers network, where one is for RGB inputs and another for partially segmented inputs and aggregating their outputs to produce precise pose and shape estimations. Experimental results demonstrate that OCCL-Former surpasses existing state-of-the-art methods, delivering superior accuracy and robustness in 3D human pose estimation under both standard and occluded conditions on standard benchmarks. The proposed OCCL-Former achieves 9.6, 9.7, and 8.4 lesser MPJPE, PA-MPJPE, and PVE error, respectively than the recent state-of-the-art approach on the popular benchmark standard 3DPW dataset.

Keywords: 3D Human Pose Estimation · 3D HPE · Shape Estimation · Transformer · OCCL-Former · Attention Mechanism · Data Augmentation · Occlusion-Aware

1 Introduction

3D human pose estimation from single images has garnered significant attention due to its broad applications in fields such as augmented reality [2],

C. Xing et al. (Eds.): METAVERSE 2024, LNCS 15429, pp. 3–14, 2025.
https://doi.org/10.1007/978-3-031-76977-1_1

human-computer interaction [3], and autonomous driving [1]. Despite considerable advancements, existing methods often encounter difficulties when dealing with occlusions, which severely affect their accuracy and robustness [1,4]. Current state-of-the-art techniques in 3D human pose estimation have demonstrated impressive performance under ideal conditions [5–7]. However, these methods tend to struggle with occlusions–situations where parts of the human body are obscured by other objects or by self-occlusion [1,6]. This is primarily because, while effective at capturing local features, it often lacks the global context required to infer occluded body parts accurately [1]. Consequently, this limitation results in suboptimal pose estimates and deteriorates the performance of these models in real-world scenarios. Recent approaches have attempted to address these challenges by incorporating various strategies, such as multi-view fusion and iterative refinement [1]. However, these methods often rely on CNN-based architecture that has a suboptimal capacity to extract inter-body part dependencies compared to the transformer architecture.

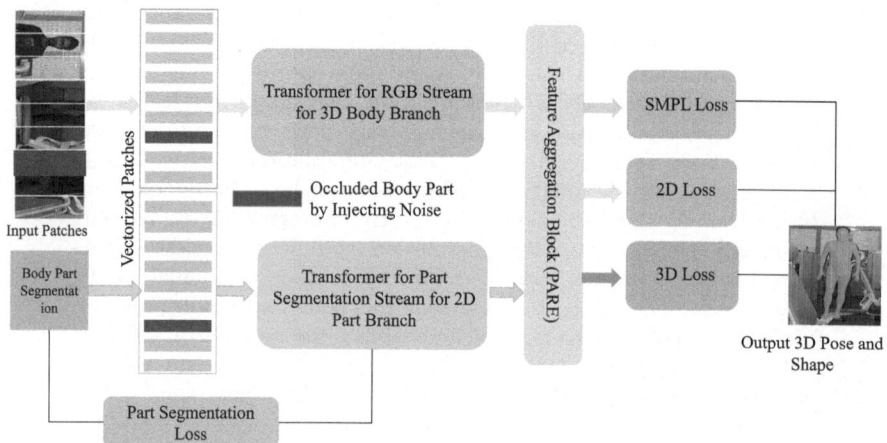

Fig. 1. Overview of the OCCL-Former Architecture. The OCCL-Former model integrates 2D part attention and 3D RGB stream for handling occlusion to achieve robust 3D human pose estimation. The input RGB image is processed in the vectorized patches steps. These processed inputs are then fed into the RGB stream. From the RGB image, we perform body part segmentation that feeds into a 2D part attention branch. The 2D part attention branch generates attention maps supervised by part segmentation labels in the initial training stages, which are later turned into pure soft attention to handle occlusions. We aggregate the feature by following the work described in PARE [1]. We provide three losses and supervision SMPL parameters, 2D loss and 3D loss. We use synthetic occlusion during training to improve the model's robustness to occlusions. The final model is trained end-to-end, leveraging both supervised and unsupervised learning phases.

In this work, we propose a novel transformer-based method, OCCL-Former, to extract these inter-body joint relationships to advance 3D human pose estimation under occlusions. Transformers, originally designed for natural language processing [8], have recently shown remarkable success in vision tasks, including image classification and object detection [9]. The self-attention mechanism of the transformers provide a robust framework for capturing long-range dependencies and global contextual information [8,9], which are crucial for handling occlusions. By treating image patches or regions as sequences, transformers can learn complex relationships and contextual cues across the entire image, potentially improving the estimation of occluded body parts. In our work, the OCCL-Former is designed to learn and leverage inter-body parts relationships by integrating global context and dependencies. Our approach consists of two key components such as, the estimation of relationships between body parts and joints, and the regression of occluded parts using visible information. This dual-stream process enables OCCL-Former to handle occlusions more effectively than existing methods. OCCL-Former employs two customized vision transformer to extract global contextual information and model complex dependencies among body parts. We exploit augmented data with simulated occlusions using the SyntheticOC approach [10] during training to enhance the model's ability to infer missing parts. By using two transformers, where one is for RGB inputs and another for partially segmented inputs, we aggregate the outputs to achieve robust and accurate pose estimations. Our method also incorporates full-body supervision during training to guide the model in learning accurate inter-joint relationships similar to the PARE [1]. Extensive experiments on benchmark datasets demonstrate that OCCL-Former significantly outperforms existing methods in terms of MPJPE, PA-MPJPE, PVE and robustness in both standard and occlusion scenarios.

Our approach not only improves the performance of 3D human pose estimation but also advances the state-of-the-art (SOTA) methods by effectively addressing the limitations posed by the occlusions. This work underscores the potential of Transformer-based architectures in overcoming the limitations of conventional methods for 3D human pose estimation. By effectively leveraging global contextual information and modeling inter-body parts relationships, our proposed OCCL-Former represents a significant step forward in achieving accurate and robust pose estimations in complex and occluded environments. Our core contribution can be summarized as:

1. Introducing OCCL-Former, a novel transformer-based method for 3D human pose estimation that effectively handles occlusions by learning and leveraging inter-body parts relationships via global contextual information.
2. Employing a two-stream process where the first stream estimates the relationships between body parts and joints in 3D, and the second stream uses the 2D part attention mechanism to regresses the occluded parts using information from visible body regions.
3. Enhancing model robustness by incorporating augmented data with simulated occlusions during training and providing full-body supervision. This enables OCCL-Former to better infer occluded body parts based on partial and noisy inputs.

4. OCCL-Former utilizes two separate transformers, one is for RGB images and another for partially segmented inputs, and integrates their outputs to achieve superior accuracy and robustness in 3D HPE.

2   Literature Review

2.1   3D Human Pose Estimation

3D human pose estimation from single images has seen substantial progress with the advent of deep learning techniques. Early methods relied heavily on 2D keypoint detection followed by triangulation approaches to estimate 3D poses. These approaches were limited by their reliance on multi-view setups and geometric assumptions [11,12]. The introduction of convolutional neural networks (CNNs) revolutionized the field by enabling end-to-end learning of 3D pose from a single image, significantly improving accuracy [13,14].

2.2   Handling Occlusions

One of the key challenges in 3D human pose estimation is handling occlusions, where body parts are obscured by other objects or the self. Early methods addressed occlusions by incorporating multi-view information or additional sensors [15]. More recent approaches have attempted to handle occlusions through advanced network architectures and data augmentation. For instance, Zhao et al. [16] introduced a multi-stage network that refines pose estimates iteratively, improving robustness to occlusions. However, these methods still struggle with complex occlusions and rely on additional data or complex processing.

2.3   Transformers in Vision

The success of transformers in natural language processing has led to their adoption in computer vision tasks. Vision Transformers (ViTs) have demonstrated remarkable performance in image classification and object detection by capturing global dependencies through self-attention mechanisms [17]. [9] first applied the transformer to vision tasks, showing that self-attention can effectively model long-range relationships. More recent works have explored the application of the transformers to pose estimation. For example, Zhang et al. [18] utilized the transformer for object detection, providing a foundation for their application in pose estimation tasks.

2.4   Occlusion Handling with Transformers

Incorporating transformers into the occlusion handling process for 3D pose estimation is relatively new. Recent studies have explored transformer-based models to address occlusions in related tasks. Li et al. [19] proposed a transformer-based approach for pose estimation that includes mechanisms for handling occlusions, demonstrating the potential for applying similar strategies in 3D pose estimation. However, these methods often lack the comprehensive integration of global context and part relationships needed for robust 3D pose estimation. However these approaches struggle to find inter-body joints dependencies perfectly [1].

Our proposed OCCL-Former addresses these limitations by integrating a transformer-based approach to model global contextual information and inter-body part relationships. Unlike previous methods, OCCL-Former combines two transformers for RGB and partially segmented inputs, providing a comprehensive solution for handling occlusions. By leveraging augmented data and simulated occlusions during training, our method significantly improves accuracy and robustness in 3D human pose estimation.

3   Proposed Methodology

Figure 1 shows the overview of our proposed approach. The OCCL-Former model addresses occlusion by integrating a 3D RGB stream with a 2D part attention method, leading to reliable 3D human pose estimation. The RGB input image is first splited into vectorized patches to start the procedure. After that, the RGB stream receives these patches for further processing. Body part segmentation is applied to the RGB image concurrently. Following segmentation, a 2D part attention branch uses this data to create attention maps. During the training phase, part segmentation labels serve as the initial supervisors for these maps. As this supervision is gradually removed, the maps become pure soft-attention, which improves the model's handling of occlusions.

Using the process outlined in PARE [1], the features from the RGB stream and the 2D part attention branch are combined. The final pose estimation is based on this aggregated feature set. The model includes three types of losses and supervisions (SMPL parameters, 2D loss, and 3D loss) to guarantee correctness and robustness. To further strengthen the model's resistance to occlusions in the real environment, artificial occlusions are included during training. In conclusion, both supervised and unsupervised learning stages are used to train the OCCL-Former model end-to-end, enabling it to perform very well in 3D human pose estimation tasks even when occlusions are present.

Let us consider, given an input image, containing a human body, our goal is to estimate the 3D pose, represented as a set of 3D joint coordinates $\mathbf{P} \in \mathbb{R}^{N \times 3}$, where N denotes the number of joints. We aim to handle occlusions by accurately estimating occluded joints based on visible information.

3.1   RGB Stream for 3D Body Part

We model the relationship between body parts using two vision transformers (ViTs). The input image is divided into non-overlapping patches of size $P \times P$. Each patch $\mathbf{x}_i$ is linearly embedded into a vector space of dimension D using a learnable projection matrix $\mathbf{W}$:

$$\mathbf{e}_i = \mathbf{W}\mathbf{x}_i \tag{1}$$

where $\mathbf{e}_i \in \mathbb{R}^D$ denotes the embedded patch representation. The sequence of patch embeddings $\{\mathbf{e}_1, \mathbf{e}_2, \ldots, \mathbf{e}_N\}$ is augmented with positional encodings $\mathbf{p}_i$ to retain spatial information:

$$\mathbf{e}'_i = \mathbf{e}_i + \mathbf{p}_i \tag{2}$$

The Transformer encoder processes these embeddings through self-attention mechanisms. The self-attention mechanism computes attention scores $\mathbf{A}_{ij}$ between patches $\mathbf{e}'_i$ and $\mathbf{e}'_j$ as follows:

$$\mathbf{A}_{ij} = \text{softmax}\left(\frac{\mathbf{Q}_i \mathbf{K}_j^\top}{\sqrt{D}}\right) \tag{3}$$

where $\mathbf{Q}_i$ and $\mathbf{K}_j$ are query and key matrices obtained from the embeddings. The output of the self-attention layer is:

$$\mathbf{z}_i = \sum_j \mathbf{A}_{ij} \mathbf{V}_j \tag{4}$$

where $\mathbf{V}_j$ denotes the value vectors. The aggregated output captures global dependencies and relationships between body parts. For the second stream that takes body part segmented input to estimate 2D part features we use the process described in PARE [1].

3.2 Aggregation of the Feature of the Transformers

To aggregate the features and obtain the desired output we have adopted the computation described in PARE [1].

3.3 Training and Loss Functions

During training we employ four loss terms such as, 1) 3D loss (L_{3D}): the Mean Per Joint Position Error (MPJPE) between the 3D output and ground truth 3D points, 2) 2D loss (L_{2D}): MPJPE error between output 2D and ground projected 2D, the projected 2D is obtained by projecting 3D points of SMPL [20], 3) SMPL loss (L_{SMPL}): MPJPE error between the output and ground truth SMPL parameters, and 4) Part Segmentation Loss (L_P): Cross entropy loss between output and ground truth 2D body part segmentation stream.

The overall loss function for training OCCL-Former is as follows:

$$\mathcal{L}_{total} = \alpha_{3D} L_{3D} + \alpha_{2D} L_{2D} + \alpha_{SMPL} L_{SMPL} + \alpha_P L_P \tag{5}$$

4 Experimental Setup

To evaluate our proposed approach we have used the identical training setup and environment similar to PARE [1]. We have evaluate our approach on two standard benchmark datasets: 1) 3DPW and 2) 3DOH.

Table 1. Performance of the proposed OCCL-Former on 3DPW dataset (lower is better). The proposed method achieves better performance than existing SOTA approaches. Bold text represents the best performance.

Methods	MPJPE ↓	PA-MPJPE ↓	PVE ↓
HMMR [21]	116.5	72.6	–
Doersch et al. [22]	–	74.7	–
Sun et al. [23]	–	69.5	–
VIBE [24]	93.5	56.5	113.4
MEVA [25]	86.9	54.7	–
Pose2Mesh [26]	89.2	58.9	–
Zanfir et al. [27]	90.0	57.1	–
I2L-MeshNet [28]	93.2	58.6	–
LearnedGD [29]	–	56.4	–
HMR [21]	130.0	76.7	–
CMR [30]	–	70.2	–
SPIN [31]	96.9	59.2	135.1
HMR-EFT [32]	–	54.2	–
PARE (R50) [1]	82.9	52.3	99.7
OCCL-Former (Ours)	**72.3**	**42.6**	**81.4**

Table 2. Performance of OCCL-Former on occlusion specific dataset 3DPW-OCC, and 3DOH (lower is better). Bold text represents the best performance.

Method	3DPW-OCC			3DOH	
	MPJPE ↓	PA-MPJPE ↓	PVE ↓	MPJPE ↓	PA-MPJPE ↓
Zhang et al. [33]	–	72.2	–	–	58.5
SPIN [31]	95.6	60.8	121.6	104.3	68.3
HMR-EFT [32]	94.4	60.9	111.3	75.2	53.1
PARE (R50) [1]	90.5	56.6	107.9	63.3	44.3
OCCL-Former (Ours)	**86.3**	**51.1**	**93.8**	**55.4**	**40.6**

5 Results and Discussion

5.1 Comparison to the State-of-the-Art

Table 1 shows the performance comparison between OCCL-Former and existing state-of-the-art single-RGB-image human pose estimation (HPE) methods. OCCL-Former achieves new state-of-the-art results. The performance is better than the existing approaches in all the metrics such as MPJPE, PA-MPJPE, and PVE by a significant margin. From Table 1, we can see that the mean per joint position error (MPJPE) of OCCL-Former is 72.3% which is significantly better than the existing works. OCCL-Former achieves 42.6%, and 81.4%, on

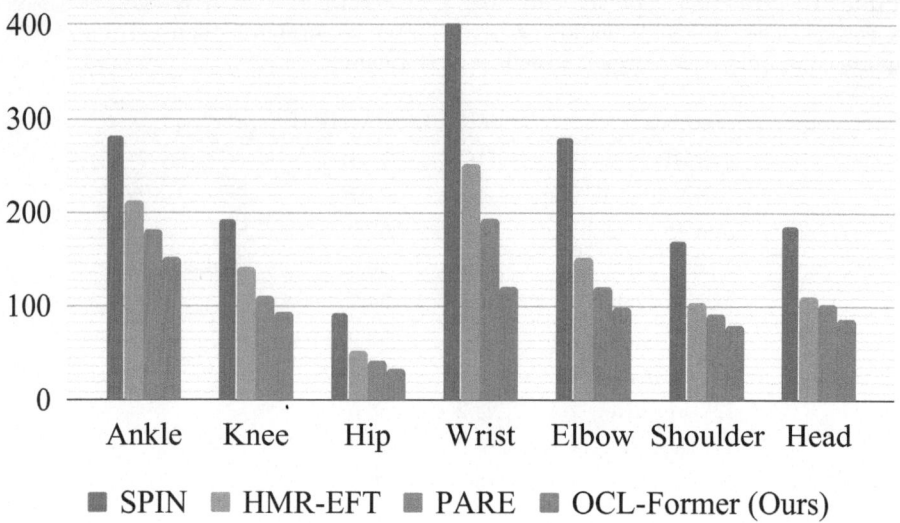

Fig. 2. Comparison between OCCL-Former and existing methods in terms of per joint sensitivity analysis. The competing results are obtained from [1]. The X-axis represents the joints and the Y-axis represents the average joint error in mm.

PA-MPJPE and PVE metrics, respectively, on the 3DPW dataset. The proposed OCCL-Former achieves 9.6, 9.7, and 8.4 lesser MPJPE, PA-MPJPE, and PVE error, respectively, than [1].

OCCL-Former performs better than the existing SOTA methods on occlusion-specific datasets as reported in Table 2. As OCCL-Former is trained using augmented data as described in Sect. 3, OCCL-Former is more robust under occlusion than existing works. Our approach achieves better performance in all the metrics for both datasets. For fair comparison, we trained Zhang et al. [33], HMREFT [32], and OCCL-Former using COCO, Human3.6M, and 3DOH by following the work described in [1]. We perform the analysis of per joint sensitivity analysis among existing methods SPIN [31], HMR-EFT [32], PARE [1], and our proposed approach OCCL-Former as shown in Fig. 2 where Y-axis indicates the average joint error in mm. During evaluation we follow the identical setup similar to [1]. From Fig. 2 we observe that our proposed approach OCCL-Former achieves lower per joint error than all the competing approaches.

5.2 Qualitative Comparison

A qualitative comparison between our proposed OCCL-Former, and PARE is shown in Fig. 3 on real world scenerios. While the PARE results show that occlusion augmentation improves robustness to occlusions, this improvement is insufficient on its own. OCCL-Former performs well even under challenging occlusion conditions by leveraging its attention mechanism.

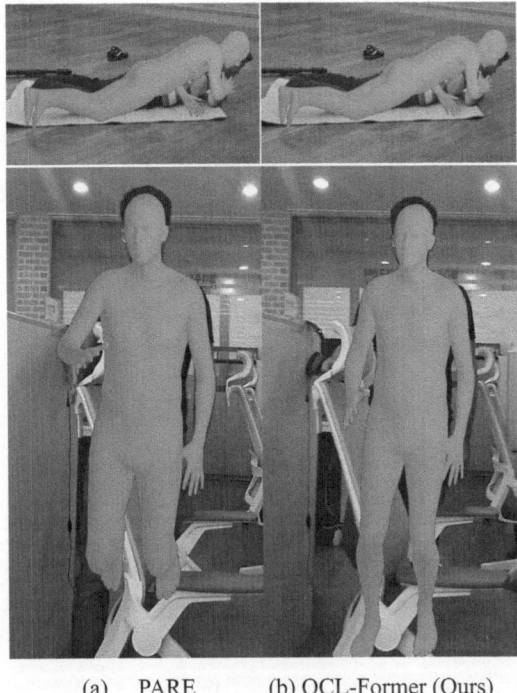

(a)   PARE   (b) OCL-Former (Ours)

Fig. 3. Visualization of the robustness on handling occlusion of real-world scenarios between PARE (a) and our proposed OCCL-Former (b).

6   Conclusion

In this paper, we proposed OCCL-Former, a transformer-based framework that addresses the challenge of occlusions in 3D human pose estimation by leveraging global contextual information and inter-body part relationships. By introducing a dual-stream process that first models body part dependencies and then regresses occluded parts, OCCL-Former significantly enhances pose accuracy and robustness. The integration of dual transformers, where one is for RGB images and another one is for partially segmented inputs further improves the performance by effectively combining visible and occluded data. Extensive experiments on benchmark datasets validate that OCCL-Former outperforms existing methods, offering a substantial advancement in handling occlusions. Our approach not only sets a new standard in pose estimation but also opens avenues for future research into refining the model and extending its application to additional contexts. However, in this work, we only focus on the performance and robustness of the OCCL-Former approach in handling occlusions. In this future work, we will analyse the complexity of OCCL-Former to propose a more lightweight approach without sacrificing performance. We will adopt our work OCCL-Former in more diverse tasks as well as real-world scenarios.

Acknowledgement. This research was supported by Culture, Sports and Tourism R&D Program through the Korea Creative Content Agency grant funded by the Ministry of Culture, Sports and Tourism in 2024 (Project Name: Development of a mobile disaster safety prevention experience platform based on tangible XR content and motion simulator, Project Number: RS-2023-002.

Competing Interests. The authors have no competing interests to declare relevant to this article's content.

Authors Contribution Statement. 1. Md. Imtiaz Hossain, as the first author, made substantial contributions to the problem statement, idea proposal, implementations, experiments, drafted the work, paper writing, conception or design of the work.

2. Sharmen Akhter, as one of the co-author, discussed the discussion of the results, revised and improved the paper writing, revised the draft critically for important intellectual content;

3. Sungjun Yang, as one of the co-authors, checked and approved the revised version of the paper.

4. *Eui-Nam Huh, as the corresponding author, supervised the work, and appropriately investigated and approved the revised version for all aspects of the work.

Ethical and Informed Consent for Data Used. Not Applicable (N/A): All the data used in this paper are publicly available and all the necessary resources are cited.

Data Availability and Access. Not Applicable (N/A)

References

1. Zhao, J., et al.: Autonomous driving system: a comprehensive survey. Expert Syst. Appl. **242**, 122836 (2023)
2. Dargan, S., Bansal, S., Kumar, M., Mittal, A., Kumar, K.: Augmented reality: a comprehensive review. Arch. Comput. Methods Eng. **30**(2), 1057–1080 (2023)
3. Kosch, T., Karolus, J., Zagermann, J., Reiterer, H., Schmidt, A., Woźniak, P.W.: A survey on measuring cognitive workload in human-computer interaction. ACM Comput. Surv. **55**(13s), 1–39 (2023)
4. Ran, H., Ning, X., Li, W., Hao, M., Tiwari, P.: 3D human pose and shape estimation via de-occlusion multi-task learning. Neurocomputing **548**, 126284 (2023)
5. Tripathi, S., Müller, L., Huang, C.-H.P., Taheri, O., Black, M.J., Tzionas, D.: 3D human pose estimation via intuitive physics. In: Proceedings of the IEEE/CVF Conference on Computer Vision and Pattern Recognition, pp. 4713–4725 (2023)
6. Zhang, Y., Ji, P., Wang, A., Mei, J., Kortylewski, A., Yuille, A.: 3D-aware neural body fitting for occlusion robust 3D human pose estimation. In: Proceedings of the IEEE/CVF International Conference on Computer Vision, pp. 9399–9410 (2023)
7. Tang, Z., Qiu, Z., Hao, Y., Hong, R., Yao, T.: 3D human pose estimation with spatio-temporal criss-cross attention. In: Proceedings of the IEEE/CVF Conference on Computer Vision and Pattern Recognition, pp. 4790–4799 (2023)
8. Vaswani, A.: Attention is all you need. arXiv preprint arXiv:1706.03762 (2017)
9. Han, K., et al.: A survey on vision transformer. IEEE Trans. Pattern Anal. Mach. Intell. **45**(1), 87–110 (2022)

10. Sárándi, I., Linder, T., Arras, K.O., Leibe, B.: How robust is 3D human pose estimation to occlusion? arXiv preprint arXiv:1808.09316 (2018)

11. Ioffe, S., Szegedy, C.: Batch normalization: accelerating deep network training by reducing internal covariate shift. In: International Conference on Machine Learning, pp. 448–456. PMLR (2015)

12. Li, S., Chan, A.B.: 3D human pose estimation from monocular images with deep convolutional neural network. In: Cremers, D., Reid, I., Saito, H., Yang, M.-H. (eds.) ACCV 2014. LNCS, vol. 9004, pp. 332–347. Springer, Cham (2015). https://doi.org/10.1007/978-3-319-16808-1_23

13. Toshev, A., Szegedy, C.: DeepPose: human pose estimation via deep neural networks. In: Proceedings of the IEEE Conference on Computer Vision and Pattern Recognition, pp. 1653–1660 (2014)

14. Girshick, R., Iandola, F., Darrell, T., Malik, J.: Deformable part models are convolutional neural networks. In: Proceedings of the IEEE Conference on Computer Vision and Pattern Recognition, pp. 437–446 (2015)

15. Xu, C., Yu, X., Wang, Z., Ou, L.: Multi-view human pose estimation in humanrobot interaction. In: IECON 2020 The 46th Annual Conference of the IEEE Industrial Electronics Society, pp. 4769–4775. IEEE (2020)

16. Zhao, Q., Zheng, C., Liu, M., Chen, C.: A single 2D pose with context is worth hundreds for 3D human pose estimation. In: Advances in Neural Information Processing Systems, vol. 36 (2024)

17. Huang, P., Kong, Z., Wang, L., Han, X., Yang, X.: Efficient and stable unsupervised feature selection based on novel structured graph and data discrepancy learning. IEEE Trans. Neural Netw. Learn. Syst., 1–15 (2024). https://doi.org/10.1109/TNNLS.2024.3385838

18. Zhang, C., Zhang, C., Guo, Y., Chen, L., Happold, M.: MotionTrack: end-to-end transformer-based multi-object tracking with lidar-camera fusion. In: Proceedings of the IEEE/CVF Conference on Computer Vision and Pattern Recognition, pp. 151–160 (2023)

19. Li, Z., Li, Y., Lin, S.: RAGT: learning robust features for occluded human pose and shape estimation with attention-guided transformer. In: Hu, SM., Cai, Y., Rosin, P. (eds.) International Conference on Computer-Aided Design and Computer Graphics, pp. 329–347. Springer, Singapore (2023). https://doi.org/10.1007/978-981-99-9666-7_22

20. Bogo, F., Kanazawa, A., Lassner, C., Gehler, P., Romero, J., Black, M.J.: Keep it SMPL: automatic estimation of 3D human pose and shape from a single image. In: Leibe, B., Matas, J., Sebe, N., Welling, M. (eds.) ECCV 2016. LNCS, vol. 9909, pp. 561–578. Springer, Cham (2016). https://doi.org/10.1007/978-3-319-46454-1_34

21. Kanazawa, A., Black, M.J., Jacobs, D.W., Malik, J.: End-to-end recovery of human shape and pose. In: Proceedings of the IEEE Conference on Computer Vision and Pattern Recognition, pp. 7122–7131 (2018)

22. Doersch, C., Zisserman, A.: Sim2real transfer learning for 3D human pose estimation: motion to the rescue. In: Advances in Neural Information Processing Systems, vol. 32 (2019)

23. Sun, Y., Ye, Y., Liu, W., Gao, W., Fu, Y., Mei, T.: Human mesh recovery from monocular images via a skeleton-disentangled representation. In: Proceedings of the IEEE/CVF International Conference on Computer Vision, pp. 5349–5358 (2019)

24. Kocabas, M., Athanasiou, N., Black, M.J.: Vibe: video inference for human body pose and shape estimation. In: Proceedings of the IEEE/CVF Conference on Computer Vision and Pattern Recognition, pp. 5253–5263 (2020)

25. Luo, Z., Golestaneh, S.A., Kitani, K.M.: 3D human motion estimation via motion compression and refinement. In: Proceedings of the Asian Conference on Computer Vision (2020)
26. Choi, H., Moon, G., Lee, K.M.: Pose2Mesh: graph convolutional network for 3D human pose and mesh recovery from a 2D human pose. In: Vedaldi, A., Bischof, H., Brox, T., Frahm, J.-M. (eds.) ECCV 2020. LNCS, vol. 12352, pp. 769–787. Springer, Cham (2020). https://doi.org/10.1007/978-3-030-58571-6_45
27. Zanfir, A., Bazavan, E.G., Xu, H., Freeman, W.T., Sukthankar, R., Sminchisescu, C.: Weakly supervised 3D human pose and shape reconstruction with normalizing flows. In: Vedaldi, A., Bischof, H., Brox, T., Frahm, J.-M. (eds.) ECCV 2020. LNCS, vol. 12351, pp. 465–481. Springer, Cham (2020). https://doi.org/10.1007/978-3-030-58539-6_28
28. Moon, G., Lee, K.M.: I2L-MeshNet: image-to-lixel prediction network for accurate 3D human pose and mesh estimation from a single RGB image. In: Vedaldi, A., Bischof, H., Brox, T., Frahm, J.-M. (eds.) ECCV 2020. LNCS, vol. 12352, pp. 752–768. Springer, Cham (2020). https://doi.org/10.1007/978-3-030-58571-6_44
29. Song, J., Chen, X., Hilliges, O.: Human body model fitting by learned gradient descent. In: Vedaldi, A., Bischof, H., Brox, T., Frahm, J.-M. (eds.) ECCV 2020. LNCS, vol. 12365, pp. 744–760. Springer, Cham (2020). https://doi.org/10.1007/978-3-030-58565-5_44
30. Kolotouros, N., Pavlakos, G., Daniilidis, K.: Convolutional mesh regression for single-image human shape reconstruction. In: Proceedings of the IEEE/CVF Conference on Computer Vision and Pattern Recognition, pp. 4501–4510 (2019)
31. Kolotouros, N., Pavlakos, G., Black, M.J., Daniilidis, K.: Learning to reconstruct 3D human pose and shape via model-fitting in the loop. In: Proceedings of the IEEE/CVF International Conference on Computer Vision, pp. 2252–2261 (2019)
32. Joo, H., Neverova, N., Vedaldi, A.: Exemplar fine-tuning for 3D human model fitting towards in-the-wild 3D human pose estimation. In: 2021 International Conference on 3D Vision (3DV), pp. 42–52. IEEE (2021)
33. Zhang, T., Huang, B., Wang, Y.: Object-occluded human shape and pose estimation from a single color image. In: Proceedings of the IEEE/CVF Conference on Computer Vision and Pattern Recognition, pp. 7376–7385 (2020)

Does Digital Transformation Affect the Financialization of Real Sector Firms?

Zhihao Yang[1] ⓘ, Xiangyu Meng[2] ⓘ, Mengting Zou[2(✉)] ⓘ, Yongping Qiu[3] ⓘ, and Jiacai Lai[4] ⓘ

[1] Postdoctoral Research Station, Agricultural Bank of China, Peking 100005, China
[2] Wuhan University of Technology, Wuhan 430070, China
zmt1130@126.com
[3] Agricultural Bank of China, Peking 100005, China
[4] Chinese Association for Artificial Intelligence, Peking 100005, China

Abstract. Worldwide, digital technologies are profoundly influencing the inner logic of a wide scope of economic activities. As the most important subjects in the market economy, firms are also deeply affected by the transformation of digital technology; moreover, they also facilitate digital technology developments and applications. Using data from A-share listed firms in China from 2007 to 2020, this study finds that digital transformation promotes the financialization of real sector firms. Specifically, testing the influence mechanism reveals that digital transformation assists in the financialization of real sector firms by alleviating firm financing constraints. A heterogeneity analysis shows that the promotion effect that digital transformation has on firm financialization is more significant in non-state-owned firms, firms in the high-tech industry, and small- and medium-sized firms. The results offer insights that may help the government formulate policies that support and promote firms' digital transformation and help firms undergo digital transformations more effectively. This is the first study to determine how digital transformation affects the financialization of non-financial firms.

Keywords: Digital Transformation · Financialization · Corporate Governance

1 Introduction

Digital technologies, represented by artificial intelligence, blockchain, cloud computing, and big data, are significantly impacting markets and daily life across the globe. Firms, the most important players in the market economy, are not only deeply impacted by transformations in digital technology, but are also involved in digital technology developments and applications [24]. In the 21st century, the rapid development of digital technology has changed the concept of "digital transformation." In the context of digitization, "transformation" broadly signifies a dynamic process that comprises process digitization, product and service digitization, and business model digitization [20]. It is important to note that "digital transformation" may be delineated from a variety of perspectives. From the perspective of organizational transformation, digital transformation involves the integration of digital technologies and business processes in the

C. Xing et al. (Eds.): METAVERSE 2024, LNCS 15429, pp. 15–32, 2025.
https://doi.org/10.1007/978-3-031-76977-1_2

digital economy [14]. The success of such transformations lies not only in the use of advanced technologies and methods, but also in adaptation and cooperation at the organizational level [8]. Meanwhile, from the perspective of innovative business models, "digital transformation" refers to the actions a firm undertakes to reshape its products, services, information, and customer engagement style, which ultimately reshape its value propositions [2]. From the perspective of assets, digital transformation is not a process that digitizes existing business operations; rather, it is a process that transforms products and services into software-defined assets and leverages these digital assets to redefine business operations [6]. From a basic technology perspective, the digital revolution and changes in the content of digitization (e.g., the use of computers, telecommunication equipment, the Internet, and the Internet of Things) have accelerated the breaking down of boundaries between different industries, formation of new business ecosystems, and establishment of partnerships between firms [21].

Although scholars have not reached a consensus on the definition of "digital transformation," most believe that firms' digital transformations have a positive impact on the economy. Scholars argue that digital transformation in firms can reduce business costs [22] and increase productivity [1], innovation [3, 7, 12], financial performance [9], and business performance [12, 16]. However, there is a lack of research on how firms' digital transformations influence their own investment decisions and financialization. Firm financialization is an important indicator of the "off real to virtual" economic process, a critical issue in economic development across the world. However, scholars have not determined how firm digital transformation affects non-financial firm financialization or the path through which it affects firm financialization. These questions deserve further research.

To examine the effect of digital transformation on the financialization of non-financial firms, we must first define firm "financialization." From the perspective of income, financialization is a new accumulation process in which firms obtain profit from financial channels instead of trade and the production of commodities [11]. From the perspective of the difference in return on investment, the huge difference between the returns on investment of the financial sector and the real sector drives the financialization of real sector [4]. In addition, from the perspective of asset allocation, the process in which a firm's financial assets increase as a proportion of total assets is the process of its financialization [5]. At the same time, the manifestations of financialization at the micro and macro levels are different. At the micro level, it manifests primarily in the shift in operation and income from the real economy to the financial field. At the macro level, it manifests primarily in the increasing importance of the financial sector compared to the real sector. The above-mentioned literature shows that scholars mainly define firm "financialization" from the perspective of asset allocation and income sources at the micro level. This study measures the financialization of firms from these two perspectives to determine the degree of firm financialization.

Based on data on Chinese listed firms from 2007 to 2020, this study conducts empirical research on the effect of digital transformation on the financialization of real sector firms and the specific mechanism through which firm digital transformation influences firm financialization. The main contributions of this study are as follows. First, it directly reveals how digital transformation influences the financialization of non-financial firms and examines the specific influence mechanism. Few studies focus on firms' financial asset allocation and financialization, which belong to the field of the "virtual economy." Second, this study enhances existing literature on the factors that affect firm financialization. This study examines the factors influencing firm financialization from the new perspective of firm digital transformation. Third, this study specifically explores how firm digital transformation impacts firm financialization using data on Chinese listed firms. Additionally, the study conducts a heterogeneity analysis on property rights and industry types to offer insights useful to policymaking.

2 Literature Review

2.1 Digital Transformation of Firms

Previous literature mainly explores the digital transformation of firms from the perspectives of influencing factors, exact processes, and economic consequences. Liu [14] explored the implementation of firms' digital transformation projects by constructing a theoretical framework of resource matching and argued that it is extremely important for top management to directly supervise a firm's digital transformation. Moreover, absolute consistency between a firm's business goals and its IT development strategy is an important factor in the success of its digital transformation. Li [13] studied how small- and medium-sized firms with limited abilities and resources completed digital transformations and found that management cognition, the management of social capital development, the establishment of a business team, and the development of organizational skills are important factors driving digital transformation. Additionally, a case study on digital transformation by Steiber [20] focusing on General Electric and Siemens Healthineers highlighted that the willingness to change, search for new feasible solutions, tests, and sustainability of widespread implementation and transformation also affect firms' digital transformations.

Firms undergoing digital transformations influenced by internal and external factors demonstrate different changes than firms undergoing more traditional kinds of transformations. For example, Li [12] found that, compared with the simple linear processes firms undergo during traditional approaches to strategy formulation and execution, digital transformation is usually an iterative and recursive learning process in which firms continue to formulate new strategies and adjust them based on their results. Furthermore, rather than forcing a fundamental change in one single step, digital transformation tends to occur incrementally. Such an evolving approach can make firms more dynamic and sustainable. In a case study on the digital transformation of three firms—ABB, CNH, and Vodafone—that had successfully completed a digital transformation with the help of Microsoft, Correani et al. [3] reported that firms should be concerned about the following issues during their digital transformations: (1) the scope of the digital transformation; (2) internal and external data sources, data platforms, and data processing technologies required for the transformation; and (3) professionals, partners, and customers.

Studies on the economic consequences of a firm's digital transformation mainly focus on productivity, business performance, innovative ability, and corporate governance. For instance, Bakhshi [1] examined the contribution of digitization capabilities to the operational productivity of 500 U.K. firms and found that one standard deviation increase in online data use is associated with an 8% increase in a firm's productivity level. Keeping other conditions constant, the firms in the top quartile of online data use were 13% more productive than firms in the same industry. Further, Mikalef and Pateli [16] revealed that firm digitalization enhances two types of agility, market capitalizing and operational adjustment agility, which, in sequence, enhance business performance. Additionally, Correani et al. [3] argued that digital transformation may have significant advantages for firms; for example, it may allow them to provide services that are more efficient, produce products that are more consistent with customer needs, and shorten their innovation process and time to market.

2.2 Literature Summary

In summary, most existing studies advise that digital transformation positively affects firms; specifically, they suggest that digital transformation improves firm productivity, business performance, innovative ability, and corporate governance. Meanwhile, although some scholars believe that financialization helps firms, most scholars hold negative views toward it. Studies on the factors affecting firm financialization at macro and micro levels have been done in many fields; however, no studies have yet considered how digital transformation affects the "off real to virtual" economic process at the micro level. Put differently, no scholarly work has yet been done on how firm digital transformation affects firm financialization and the specific influence mechanism in this relationship. Digitization and financialization are two important trends in firm development; therefore, exploring their inner relationship and influence mechanism is necessary to uncover important insights applicable to theory and practice on the topic. Table 1 describes the differences between this work and the previous ones.

Table 1. Literature Summary.

Previous Work	The Work
Most believe that firms' digital transformations have a positive impact on the economy	Digital transformation promotes financialisation of businesses, leading to risk
Existing literature provides evidence of positive effects in terms of economic and social benefit dimensions	The study of digital transformation moves from the level of information governance to the level of production operations
Financialisation has the role of a reservoir	Financialisation runs the risk of overfinancing the real economy

3 Theoretical Analysis and Research Hypotheses

The digital transformation of firms may promote their financialization by alleviating their financing constraints. First, it is important to recall that "digital transformation" refers to the actions a firm takes using digital technology to change its business model and reshape its products, services, and information to strengthen its interactions and collaborations with customers [2]. This process increases the transparency of a firm's information; that is, a firm's digital transformation reduces its own information asymmetry. Therefore, it is necessary to disclose relevant information to external information users, and managers must be able to reduce information uncertainty and asymmetry and increase transparency. Here, it is helpful to note that banks are the main financing sources for firms and that firms are motivated to disclose relevant information when borrowing from banks. Digital technology can help firms improve their level of information transparency. Therefore, digital transformation can reduce information asymmetries between banks and firms, thereby alleviating firm financing constraints. In addition, undergoing a digital transformation can improve a firm's financial performance [9], which also helps alleviate financing constraints.

The digital revolution has promoted the formation of new business ecosystems and establishment of partnerships between firms [21]. Along these lines, firms undergoing digital transformations often interact and collaborate with partners [3]. Regardless of whether firms join a new business ecosystem or deepen their collaborative relationships with their existing partners, digital transformations can help firms expand their financing channels beyond upstream and downstream industry chain partners or other partners and in turn alleviate their own financing constraints.

Scholars popularly suggest that firms undergo financialization for two reasons. First, they reason that precautionary motives push firms to allocate financial assets in advance to liquidate them to guarantee cash flows under financial distress. When firms are driven by precautionary motives, the alleviation of financing constraints will not give them extra incentives to allocate more financial assets. Second, arbitrage motives push firms to allocate more financial assets for high returns. When firms are driven by arbitrage motives, the alleviation of financing constraints will cause firms to allocate more financial assets for high returns. In other words, the alleviation of financing constraints will promote the financialization of firms.

To summarize, the digital transformation of firms under arbitrage motives may promote the financialization of firms by alleviating the financing constraints. We thus propose the following hypothesis. Hypothesis H1a: When other conditions remain unchanged, a firm's digital transformation positively affects its financialization; that is, digital transformation increases the degree of financialization.

When considering the impact of digital transformation on financialization, studies have found that firms need to carefully consider their own organizational structure and corporate governance from a strategic perspective in the process of digital transformation. For example, Liu et al. [15] identified digital transformation as a type of organizational transformation that integrates digital technologies and business processes in the digital economy, while Heilig et al. [8], who also approached digital transformation from an organizational perspective, concluded that the success of a digital transformation lies not only in using advanced technologies and methods, but also in organizational adaptation and cooperation. Notably, scholars suggest that when a firm's digital transformation increases its governance quality, it may inhibit firm financialization. Specifically, previous research has shown that a firm's governance quality is negatively related to the high-risk financial assets it holds; that is, a firm with higher quality governance is less likely to hold financial assets. Meanwhile, previous empirical studies have shown that digital transformations make firm governance more innovative and, relatedly, improve the quality of corporate governance by decreasing information asymmetry and irrational management. Therefore, organizational structure and corporate governance may influence the impact of digital transformation on firm financialization.

Meanwhile, firm resources and, relatedly, performance, also play a role in how digital transformation impacts financialization. From the perspective of firm resources, firms must consider internal and external data sources, platforms, and processing technologies [3] when implementing a digital transformation; this requires firms to invest in related resources. In addition, firms must use resources to hire or train professionals who can support digital transformation. If the total resources of a firm are unchanged, management will decrease the firm's investments in financial assets. Furthermore, as noted above, digital transformation increases a firm's productivity [1], enables it to provide more efficient services and products more consistent with customer needs, quickens its innovation, shortens its time to market [3], and increases its market adaptability, thereby increasing business performance [16]. The upshot is that digital transformation enhances the performance of real-economy businesses, which disincentivizes firms from investing in financial assets. Additionally, when total resources are limited, firms that seek to maximize profit allocate more resources to real-economy businesses and fewer resources to financial assets, thereby inhibiting their financialization. We thus propose the following hypothesis. Hypothesis H1b: When other conditions remain unchanged, a firm's digital transformation negatively affects its financialization; that is, digital transformation decreases the degree of financialization.

4   Research Design

4.1   Sample Selection and Data Sources

This study uses data on A-share listed firms in China from 2007 to 2020 for its initial study samples. The initial samples are screened as follows: (1) listed firms with ST or PT statuses are eliminated from the sample observations; (2) listed firms in the financial industry of the real estate industry according to the 2012 industrial classification of China Securities Regulatory Commission are eliminated from the sample observations; (3) the smallest time unit in the empirical research of this study is one year. Other than the annual data, other sample observations with one quarter or one month as their units are eliminated; (4) sample observations of listed firms without key indicators are eliminated; and (5) financial asset data are important measures of this study. As the domestic accounting standards that stipulate the new definitions and classifications of financial assets were introduced in 2007, the earliest samples included in this study are from 2007. After screening the data, a total of 24,487 firm-year observations are obtained. We obtain financial and stock market data from the Chinese Stock Market Accounting Research (CSMAR) and Chinese Research Data Services (CNRDS) databases. To prevent the influence of extreme values, we winsorize the data at the 1% and 99% levels.

4.2 Model Setting and Variable Definitions

This study proposes the research hypothesis, H1a—firm digital transformation promotes firm financialization—and its opposite hypothesis, H1b—firm digital transformation inhibits firm financialization. With reference to Liu et al. [15], we test H1a and H1b and construct the following main regression model to empirically analyze how firm digital transformation impacts firm financialization.

$$Fin_{it} = \beta_0 + \beta_1 Dig_{it} + \Sigma Controls + \Sigma Firm + \Sigma Year + \varepsilon_{it} \tag{1}$$

where *Fin* denotes the degree of a firm's financialization. With reference to Peng et al. [17], we measure a firm's financialization based on how many financial assets it holds, which we define as the proportion of total assets comprised of quasi-financial assets (e.g., trading financial assets, buying back the sale of financial assets, available-for-sale financial assets, loans and advances, and held-to-maturity investments) at the end of the period. Here, *Dig* denotes the degree of the firm's digital transformation, which we measure using the digital transformation degree index constructed by Wu et al. [23] in the CSMAR database. Unlike previous studies that used a "0–1" dummy variable that indicated "whether the firm has conducted digital transformation in the year" to measure the digital transformation of the firm, we use a more scientific and reasonable index and reflect the degree of the digital transformation of firms in a more comprehensive way. Specifically, we draw on Wu et al.'s [23] division of firm digital transformation into the use of basic technologies and the practical applications of technologies. The use of basic technologies includes four mainstream technical directions; namely, artificial intelligence, blockchain, cloud computing, and big data. The practical applications of technologies focus on their specific digital applications in business scenarios. We construct an index system for firm digital transformation inspired by these divisions by establishing feature maps in five sub-categories and matching them with the text in the firms' annual reports to form a final aggregated word frequency. Because such data are typically right-skewed, we transform the word frequency using a logarithmic function before using it to measure the degree of firm digital transformation. We select control variables according to the researched issues and specific situation of the sample. We also draw on the variables selected in Liu et al. [15], Ke et al. [10], and Wu et al. [23]. Table 2 describes the meanings, symbols, and calculation methods we use for each variable.

Table 2. Variable Definitions.

	Meaning of the variable	Symbol of the variable	Calculation method of the variable
Dependent variable	Financialization degree of the firm	*Fin*	*FIN* = quasi-financial assets/total assets at the end of the period
Independent variable	Digital transformation degree of the firm	*Dig*	Digital transformation degree of the firm in the year

(continued)

Table 2. (*continued*)

	Meaning of the variable	Symbol of the variable	Calculation method of the variable
Lagged independent variable	Lagged variable of the digital transformation degree of the firm	*Lag1.Dig*	Digital transformation degree of the firm in the current year that is lagged by one period
Control variables	Firm size	*Size*	*Size* = ln (total assets of the firm at the end of the period)
	Liability-to-asset ratio	*Lev*	*Lev* = total liabilities of the firm at the end of the period/total assets of the firm at the end of the period
	Total return on equity	*Roe*	*Roe* = the listed firm's net profit at the end of the period/owners' equity of the firm
	Growth rate of total operating income	*Growth*	Growth rate of total operating income of the listed firm
	Firm's relative value	*Bm*	*Bm* = shareholders' equity/aggregate market value
	Nature of property rights	*Soe*	1 if the firm is a state-owned firm, 0 otherwise
	Shareholding ratio of the largest shareholder	*Big*	Ratio of shares held by the largest shareholder of the listed firm
	CEO Duality	*Con*	1 if the role of chairman and general manager are taken up by the same person, 0 otherwise
	Board size	*Board*	*Board* = ln (number of board members)
	Number of years of establishment	*Age*	The number of years from the listing of the firm to the end of the current accounting period
	Shareholding ratio of institutional investors	*Ins*	Ratio of shares held by the institutional investors of the listed firms
	Operating cash flow	*Cfo*	*Cfo* = net cash flow from operations/total assets
	Industry	*Industry*	*The Guidelines for the Industrial Classification of Listed Firms* (2012), China Securities Regulatory Commission
	Year	*Year*	Control for year fixed effects

5 Empirical Results

5.1 Descriptive Statistics

Table 3 reports the descriptive statistics of the major variables. Compared with previous literature, the variables are all within a reasonable value range.

Table 3. Descriptive Statistics.

Variable	Mean	Standard deviation	Max	Lower quartile	Median	Upper quartile
Fin	0.025	0.059	0.342	0.000	0.001	0.019
Dig	1.016	1.311	4.754	0.000	0.000	1.792
Size	22.135	1.245	26.059	21.226	21.952	22.840
Lev	0.416	0.194	0.841	0.261	0.413	0.563
Roe	0.069	0.102	0.308	0.034	0.071	0.115
Growth	0.166	0.342	1.957	−0.009	0.112	0.266
Bm	0.445	0.293	1.556	0.234	0.373	0.574
Soe	0.395	0.489	1.000	0.000	0.000	1.000
Big	0.349	0.148	0.740	0.232	0.330	0.450
Con	0.261	0.439	1.000	0.000	0.000	1.000
Board	2.142	0.201	2.708	1.946	2.197	2.197
Age	10.338	6.653	27.000	5.000	9.000	15.000
Ins	0.445	0.247	0.910	0.240	0.470	0.643
Cfo	0.053	0.066	0.242	0.013	0.051	0.092

5.2 Benchmark Regression Results

Table 4 presents the empirical regression results of the effect of firm digital transformation on firm financialization. Specifically, Column (1) shows the results of the regression without the control variables, Column (2) shows the results with the control variables when controlling for individual fixed effects, and Column (3) shows the results with the control variables when controlling for both individual fixed effects and year fixed effects. The regression results of Columns (1), (2), and (3) all show that the coefficient of firm digital transformation (*Dig*) is positive and significant at the 1% level. This indicates that firm digital transformation has a significant promotive effect on firm financialization. This result is statistically and economically significant. Therefore, it supports our research hypothesis, H1a, that firm digital transformation promotes firm financialization.

Table 4. Firm Digital Transformation and Financialization.

Variable	(1)	(2)	(3)
	Fin	Fin	Fin
Dig	0.002***	0.003***	0.002***
	(5.28)	(7.49)	(4.84)
Constant	0.021***	−0.041**	−0.067***
	(13.75)	(−2.18)	(−3.28)
Sample observations	24487	24 487	24 487
Control variables	Yes	Yes	Yes
Individual fixed effects	Yes	Yes	Yes
Year fixed effect	Yes	No	Yes
Adj R^2	0.467	0.465	0.472

Note: ***, **, and * indicate significance at the 1%, 5%, and 10% levels, respectively. Values in parentheses are T-values; control variables have been omitted; the same is true for the tables below.

5.3 Analysis of the Influence Mechanism

The above empirical results prove that firm digital transformation promotes firm financialization. Meanwhile, the above discussion suggests that digital transformation may alleviate the financing constraints on firms because it can optimize the financial performance of firms and expand their financing channels by empowering them to decrease information uncertainty and asymmetry, which promotes their financialization. We construct the following model to test this influence mechanism:

$$Fc_{it} = \beta_0 + \beta_1 Dig_{it} + \Sigma Controls + \Sigma Firm + \Sigma Year + \varepsilon_{it} \qquad (2)$$

$$Fin_{it} = \beta_0 + \beta_1 Dig_{it} + \beta_2 Fc_{it} + \Sigma Controls + \Sigma Firm + \Sigma Year + \varepsilon_{it} \qquad (3)$$

Fc in Models (2) and (3) denotes the degree of firm financing constraints, which we measure with the Fc index used by previous research [18]. A larger index represents a higher degree of financing constraints. We use Model (2) to test the effect of firm digital transformation on the degree of firm financing constraints and Model (3) to test the effect of the degree of firm financing constraints on the degree of firm financialization. In Table 5, Column (1) shows the results of the regression for the effect of firm digital transformation on the degree of firm financing constraints. The coefficient of Dig is − 0.004 and is significant at the 1% level, which means that firm digital transformation significantly alleviates firm financing constraints. Column (2) shows the results of the regression for the effect of firm financing constraints on the degree of firm financialization. The coefficient of Fc is −0.064 and is significant at the 1% level, while the coefficient of Dig is 0.002 and is also significant at the 1% level. These findings evidence that the higher the degree of firm financing constraints, the lower the degree of financialization; moreover, firm financing constraints significantly inhibit firm financialization. In sum, firm digital transformation promotes firm financialization by alleviating financing constraints.

Table 5. Firm Financing Constraints.

Variable	(1)	(2)
	Fc	Fin
Fc		−0.064***
		(−20.55)
Dig	−0.004***	0.002***
	(−3.89)	(3.37)
Control variables	Yes	Yes
Sample observations	24487	24 487
Individual fixed effects	Yes	Yes
Year fixed effect	Yes	Yes
Adj R^2	0.859	0.513

Table 6. Profits from Real-economy Businesses.

Variable	(1)	(2)
	Profit	Fin
Profit		−0.040***
		(−6.58)
Dig	−0.002***	0.002***
	(−4.24)	(4.29)
Control variables	Yes	Yes
Sample observations	24487	24487
Individual fixed effects	Yes	Yes
Year fixed effect	Yes	Yes
Adj R^2	0.503	0.501

As noted above, during a digital transformation, a firm must consider internal and external data sources, platforms, and processing technologies [3]. In addition to digital technologies, physical equipment, and the funds used for training professionals, organizational adaptation and cooperation are also crucial [8]. Therefore, during a digital transformation, a firm must focus on investments and making corresponding adjustments to its organizational structures. However, these changes may adversely impact a firm's non-financial real-economy businesses, which may decrease its profits from non-financial channels during its transformation. Accordingly, firms that earn lower profits from real economy businesses may attempt to increase their profits from financial channels during a transformation by increasing their financial investments; that is, by increasing their degree of financialization. Ultimately, this strategy helps firms avoid large fluctuations in operating profits. Firms that earn greater profits from real-economy businesses have relatively low incentives to increase their profits from financial channels. Driven by the goal of profit maximization, they are more likely to invest more in real-economy businesses; that is, they will have a lower degree of financialization. We construct the following model to test this influence mechanism.

$$Profit_{it} = \beta_0 + \beta_1 Dig_{it} + \Sigma Controls + \Sigma Firm + \Sigma Year + \varepsilon_{it} \qquad (4)$$

$$Fin_{it} = \beta_0 + \beta_1 Dig_{it} + \beta_2 Profit_{it} + \Sigma Controls + \Sigma Firm + \Sigma Year + \varepsilon_{it} \qquad (5)$$

Profit in Models (4) and (5) denotes the profits of a firm from real-economy businesses. With reference to existing literature, we use relevant data from income statements to measure *Profit*, with *Profit* = (operating profits-investment income-gains or losses from changes in fair values-net exchange gains)/total assets of the firm at the end of the period. We use Model (4) to test the effect of firm digital transformation on firm real-economy business profits. Meanwhile, we use Model (5) to test the impact of firm real-economy business profits on the degree of firm financialization. These findings show that the higher the profits of a firm from its real-economy businesses, the lower its degree of financialization. Firms, driven by the goal of maximizing profit, will be more inclined to invest more resources in real-economy businesses and fewer resources in financial assets if they earn higher profits from real-economy businesses; that is, earning higher profits from real-economy businesses decreases a firm's degree of financialization. In sum, during a digital transformation, both a firm's investments and its corresponding adjustments to its organizational structures may adversely impact (i.e., decrease the profits of) its non-financial, real-economy businesses. To avoid large fluctuations in operating profits, firms that earn low profits from real-economy businesses may attempt to increase their profits from financial channels by increasing their investments in financial assets; that is, by increasing their degree of financialization (Table 6).

5.4 Further Research

In analyzing the influence mechanism, we find that digital transformation adversely affects firm real-economy profits and that firms are accordingly inclined to increase their investments in financial assets to avoid large fluctuations in operating profits. Based on this, we extensively research whether digital transformation actually increases the ratio of profits earned by firms from financial channels. With reference to Ke et al. [10], we use two indicators; namely, the ratio of profits earned from financial channels in a narrow sense and the ratio of profits earned from financial channels in a broad sense. We denote the ratio of profits earned from financial channels in a narrow sense by Ratio 1, where Ratio 1 = (investment income + gains or losses from changes in fair values + net exchange gains–investment income of associated firms or joint ventures–operating profits)/absolute value of operating profits. We denote the ratio of profits earned from financial channels in the broad sense by Ratio 2, where Ratio 2 = (investment income + gains or losses from changes in fair values + net exchange gains–operating profits)/absolute value of operating profits. Columns (1) and (2) in Table 7 show the benchmark regressions of firm digital transformation on the indicators of the ratio of profits earned from financial channels, Ratio 1 and Ratio 2. The results show that firm digital transformation significantly increases the ratio of profits earned by firms from financial channels.

Table 7. Ratio of Profits Earned by Firms from Financial Channels.

Variable	(1)	(2)
	Fin1	*Fin2*
Dig	0.117*	0.117*
	(1.79)	(1.65)
Constant	12.353***	12.274**
	(2.61)	(2.56)
Control variables	Yes	Yes
Sample observations	24 487	24 487
Individual fixed effects	Yes	Yes
Year fixed effect	Yes	Yes
Adj R^2	0.003	0.003

6   Robustness Test

6.1   Transformed Calculation Method

Method 1: Testing the Sub-categories of Firm Digital Transformation. Our word frequencies for basic technologies includes four mainstream technical directions: namely, artificial intelligence, blockchain, cloud computing, and big data. We use a logarithmic function to transform them into four indicators: *Dig 1, Dig 2, Dig 3*, and *Dig 4*. Method 2: Substitution of the Firm Financialization Indicator. With reference to Song and Lu [19] and Peng et al. [17], we include deriva-tive financial assets in firm quasi-financial assets to construct the firm financiali-zation indicator, where *Fin1* = (trading financial assets + derivative financial assets + buying back the sale of financial assets + available-for-sale financial as-sets + loans and advances + held-to-maturity investments)/total assets at the end of the period. Method 3: Endogeneity Analysis. Using explanatory variables with a 1-period lag, we re-run the benchmark regression. We also adopt the instrumental variable method. Using the mean digital transformation of the industry (*Mean.Dig*) and digital transformation with a 2-period lag (*Lag2.Dig*) as the instrumental variables, we run two regressions with a two-stage least squares (2SLS) approach. The calculations are omitted due to space limitations of the article and the results of all robustness tests support the main hypothesis.

6.2 Heterogeneity Analysis

The promotion effect of firm digital transformation on firm financialization may vary across firms with different characteristics. In response, we analyze the heterogeneity of our research samples using empirical tests to identify the differences between firms with different characteristics. This allows our study to yield more specific insights relevant to policymaking. According to the nature of property rights, we divide the firms into state-owned and non-state-owned firms. In addition, we divide the firms into high-tech and non-high-tech industries. Moreover, we divide the firms into large firms and small and medium firms based on whether a firm's size is above or below the industry mean. The regression results by groups of property rights are shown in Column (1)–(3) of Table 8. There is a significant difference between the state-owned and non-state-owned firm groups, and the promotion effect of digital transformation on firm financialization is more significant in non-state-owned firms. We argue that state-owned firms have inherent advantages in financing compared with non-state-owned firms; therefore, state-owned firms have weaker financing constraints. Accordingly, the influence mechanism by which digital transformation promotes firm financialization by alleviating firm financing constraints is less likely to affect state-owned firms. In addition, compared with non-state-owned firms, state-owned firms face less pressure from market competition and are less willing to undertake a digital transformation based on their own initiative. At the same time, they face stricter financial supervision; hence, the positive effect of digital transformation on state-owned firm financialization is relatively weak.

Meanwhile, Columns (1)–(3) of Table 9 show the regression results by high-tech and non-high-tech industries. Indicating that digital transformation has a significant promotion effect on the financialization of firms in high-tech industries, but an insignificant promotion effect on the financialization of firms in non-high-tech industries. In addition, the coefficient of the interaction term ($Dig*Ht$) is positive and significant at the 1% level, indicating that the promotion effect of digital transformation is more significant in the high-tech industry group. We maintain that although technological innovation is the core competitive edge of high-tech firms, it is not necessarily the focus of non-high-tech firms. Digital transformation is at the forefront of innovation and can only be implemented adequately if a firm has a good technical foundation and sufficient talents. Compared with non-high-tech firms, high-tech firms are more willing and able to successfully complete digital transformations; hence, the effect of digital transformation on high-tech firms is more significant.

The regression results by firm size are shown in Columns (1)–(3) of Table 10. Column (3) shows that the coefficient of the interaction term ($Dig*Small$) is negative and significant at the 1% level. These findings indicate that there is a significant difference between the large firm group and small and medium firm group and that the promotion effect of digital transformation on firm financialization is more significant in small and medium firms. The success of digital transformation lies not only in using advanced technologies and methods, but also in adaptation at the organizational level. Compared with large firms with more complex and stable organizational structures, the organizational structure of small and medium firms may more flexibly adapt to the changes brought about by digital transformation; hence, such transformation can profoundly change these firms. Accordingly, we expect the effect of digital transformation to be more significant in small and medium firms.

Table 8. Grouping by Nature of Property Rights.

Variable	(1)	(2)	(3)
	State-owned firm group	Non-state-owned firm group	
Dig	0.001*	0.002***	0.004***
	(1.68)	(2.50)	(6.91)
Soe			0.002
			(0.75)
Dig*Soe			−0.005***
			(−6.10)
Control variables	Yes	Yes	Yes
Sample observations	9981	15256	24487
Individual fixed effects	Yes	Yes	Yes
Year fixed effect	Yes	Yes	Yes
Adj R^2	0.626	0.453	0.501

Table 9. Grouping by Industry.

Variable	(1)	(2)	(3)
	High-tech industry group	Non-high-tech industry group	
Dig	0.003***	0.001	0.000
	(4.22)	(1.41)	(0.16)
Ht			−0.003
			(−1.40)
Dig*Ht			0.003***
			(4.33)
Control variables	Yes	Yes	Yes
Sample observations	13082	11405	24487
Individual fixed effects	Yes	Yes	Yes
Year fixed effect	Yes	Yes	Yes
Adj R^2	0.458	0.562	0.500

Table 10. Grouping by Firm Sizes.

Variable	(1)	(2)	(3)
	Large firm group	Small and medium firm group	
Dig	0.001*	0.002***	0.000
	(1.67)	(2.94)	(0.13)
Small			−0.006
			(−3.85)
Dig*Small			0.004***
			(6.46)
Control variables	Yes	Yes	Yes
Sample observations	10735	13752	24487
Individual fixed effects	Yes	Yes	Yes
Year fixed effect	Yes	Yes	Yes
Adj R^2	0.623	0.491	0.501

7 Conclusion

Based on data on A-share listed firms in China from 2007 to 2020, this study adopts an empirical research method to examine the influence of digital transformation on the financialization of real sector firms and to test the specific mechanism of this influence. The empirical results show that digital transformation promotes firm financialization. Meanwhile, a test of the influence mechanism shows that digital transformation promotes firm financialization by alleviating financing constraints. Furthermore, a heterogeneity analysis shows that the accelerating effect of digital transformation on firm financialization is more significant in non-state-owned firms, firms in the high-tech industry, and small- and medium-sized firms.

Based on these conclusions, we present the following policy suggestions. (1) When the government attempts to support and accelerate firm digital transformation through policies, it should provide more subsidies and rewards to enhance firm productivity and operational and innovation capacity as well as supports that encourage firms to focus on the development of real-economy businesses. Systematic supervision is also necessary to regulate the excessive financialization of firms undergoing digital transformations, to prevent firms from adopting "off real to virtual" during their digital transformations, and to actively encourage firms to increase their core business competitiveness through digital transformation. (2) When formulating policies for the digital economy, the government should develop different policies for different groups. Considering the characteristics of different types of firms in different industries with different property rights and governance structures, more specific policies should be formulated to better help firms in different fields undergo digital transformations according to their own situations to maximize the efficiency of digitalization. (3) Digital technology, as a product of the natural evolution of the digital age, will not only impact Chinese enterprises, but also enterprises in other countries will be affected by changes in the information and technological environment. At the same time, the adoption of this technology by enterprises will have an impact on their own investment behaviour, the financialisation of enterprises is a global issue with universality and commonality around the world, and as a way of choosing the investment behaviour of enterprises and the asset allocation mode, which will be affected by the financing environment at the same time, the intensification of the digital transformation on the financialisation of enterprises has a certain international research value.

Conflicts of Interest. The authors have no competing interests to declare that are relevant to the content of this article.

References

1. Bakhshi, H., Bravo-Biosca, A., Mateos-Garcia, J.: The analytical firm: estimating the effect of data and online analytics on firm performance. Nesta Working Paper **14**(5) (2014). https://www.nesta.org.uk/wp14-05/
2. Berman, S.J.: Digital transformation: opportunities to create new business models. Strategy Leadersh **40**(2), 16–24 (2012). https://doi.org/10.1108/10878571211209314
3. Correani, A., De Massis, A., Frattini, F., Petruzzelli, A.M., Natalicchio, A.: Implementing a digital strategy: learning from the experience of three digital transformation projects. Calif. Manag. Rev. **62**(4), 37–56 (2020). https://doi.org/10.1177/0008125620934864
4. Demir, F.: Capital market imperfections and financialization of real sectors in emerging markets: private Investment and cash flow relationship revisited. World Dev. **37**(5), 953–964 (2009). https://doi.org/10.1016/j.worlddev.2008.09.003
5. Dore, R.: Financialization of the global economy. Ind. Corp. Chang. **17**(6), 1097–1112 (2008). https://doi.org/10.1093/icc/dtn041
6. Duchin, R., Gilbert, T., Harford, J., Hrdlicka, C.: Precautionary savings with risky assets: when cash is not cash. J. Finance **72**(2), 793–852 (2017). https://doi.org/10.1111/jofi.12490
7. Frynas, J.G., Mol, M.J., Mellahi, K.: Management innovation made in China: Haier's Rendanheyi. Calif. Manag. Rev. **61**(1), 71–93 (2018). https://doi.org/10.1177/0008125618790244
8. Heilig, L., Lalla-Ruiz, E., Voß, S.: Digital transformation in maritime ports: analysis and a game theoretic framework. Econ. Res. Electron. Netw. **18**(2–3), 227–254 (2017). https://doi.org/10.1007/s11066-017-9122-x
9. Jeffers, P.I., Muhanna, W., Nault, B.R.: Information technology and process performance: an empirical investigation of the interaction between IT and non-IT resources. Decis. **39**(4), 703–735 (2008). https://doi.org/10.1111/j.1540-5915.2008.00209.x
10. Ke, Y., Li, Y., Wu, X.: Controlling shareholder's equity pledge and corporate investment: from the perspective of financial investment and real investment. Financ. Trade Econ. (Chinese) **40**(4), 50–66 (2019)
11. Krippner, G.R.: The financialization of the American economy. Socioecon. Rev. **3**(2), 173–208 (2005). https://doi.org/10.1093/SER/mwi008
12. Li, F.: Leading digital transformation: three emerging approaches for managing the transition. Int. J. Oper. Prod. **40**(6), 809–817 (2020). https://doi.org/10.1108/IJOPM-04-2020-0202
13. Li, L., Su, F., Zhang, W., Mao, J.Y.: Digital transformation by SME entrepreneurs: a capability perspective. Inf. Syst. J. **28**(6), 1129–1157 (2018). https://doi.org/10.1111/isj.12153

14. Liu, D., Chen, S., Chou, T.: Resource fit in digital transformation: lessons learned from the CBC bank global e-banking project. Manag. Decis. **49**(10), 1728–1742 (2011). https://doi.org/10.1108/00251741111183852
15. Liu, S., Liu, J., Yang, Y., Yang, S.: Corporate social responsibility and corporate financialization: a financial tool or management tool. Account. Res. (Chinese) **9**, 57–64 (2019)
16. Mikalef, P., Pateli, A.: Information technology-enabled dynamic capabilities and their indirect effect on competitive performance: findings from PLS-SEM and fsQCA. J. Bus. Res. **70**, 1–16 (2017). https://doi.org/10.1016/j.jbusres.2016.09.004
17. Peng, Y., Han, X., Li, J.: Economic policy uncertainty and corporate financialization. China Ind. Econ. (Chinese) **1**, 137–155 (2018). https://doi.org/10.19581/j.cnki.ciejournal.201801 15.010
18. Oluk, J., Kammerlander, N.: Digital transformation in family-owned mittelstand firms: a dynamic capabilities perspective. Eur. J. Innov. Manag. **30**(6), 676–711 (2021). https://doi.org/10.1080/0960085X.2020.1857666
19. Song, J., Lu, Y.: U-shape relationship between non-currency financial assets and operating profit: evidence from financialization of Chinese Listed non-financial corporates. Financ. Res. (Chinese) **6**, 111–127 (2015)
20. Steiber, A., Alänge, S., Ghosh, S., Goncalves, D.: Digital transformation of industrial firms: an innovation diffusion perspective. Eur. J. Innov. Manag. **24**(3), 799–819 (2021). https://doi.org/10.1108/EJIM-01-2020-0018
21. Teece, D.J.: Profiting from innovation in the digital economy: enabling technologies, standards, and licensing models in the wireless world. Res. Policy **47**(8), 1367–1387 (2018). https://doi.org/10.1016/j.respol.2017.01.015
22. Vial, G.: Understanding digital transformation: a review and a research agenda. J. Strateg. Inf. Syst. **28**(2), 118–144 (2019). https://doi.org/10.1016/j.jsis.2019.01.003
23. Wu, F., Hu, H., Lin, H., Ren, X.: Firm digital transformation and capital market performance: empirical evidence from stock liquidity. Manag. World (Chinese) **37**(7), 130–144 (2021). https://doi.org/10.19744/j.cnki.11-1235/f.2021.0097
24. Zhu, L.: Deep integration of artificial intelligence and manufacturing: connotation mechanism and path. Rural Financ. Res. **8**, 60–69 (2023). https://doi.org/10.16127/j.cnki.issn1003-1812.2023.08.003

Insights into the High-Quality Development of Agriculture under the Wave of Digital Economy

Liang ChaoYu[1], Wu XiangQiong[2(✉)], Ou Hui[2], and Liang Shengping[3]

[1] College of Information Engineering, Capital Normal University, Beijing 100048, China
[2] College of Mathematics and Statistics, Hunan Normal University, Changsha 410081, China
16601033305@163.com
[3] China Forestry Group Corporation, Beijing 100026, China

Abstract. Based on panel data from 30 provinces, autonomous regions, and municipalities in China from 2012 to 2021, this study conducted a quantitative analysis of the high-quality development of agriculture amidst the wave of the digital economy. The research revealed that the digital economy plays a significant role in promoting the high-quality development of agriculture. It not only directly enhances the high-quality development of agriculture in various provinces, autonomous regions, and municipalities but also indirectly provides a material foundation for such development by elevating the level of agricultural talent cultivation. However, the impact of the digital economy on the high-quality development of agriculture exhibits regional heterogeneity, with notable effects in the northern region and less significant impacts in the southern region. Consequently, this study's analysis points out that strengthening strategies to empower agriculture with the digital economy, optimizing talent attraction and cultivation mechanisms, and enhancing differentiated policy support are crucial strategies for promoting the high-quality development of agriculture.

Keywords: Agricultural High-Quality Development · Digital Economy · Two-way Fixed Effects Model · Regional Heterogeneity

1 Introduction

The report of the 20th National Congress of the Communist Party of China highlights that high-quality development is the primary task in comprehensively building a modern socialist country, emphasizing the priority of agricultural and rural development and accelerating the construction of an agricultural powerhouse [1]. As the cornerstone of the national economy, agriculture, cornerstone of national economy, underpins stability, prosperity & shapes new development paradigm. Its growth ties to social harmony & national welfare. In this context, digital transformation of agriculture is imperative for digital economy's high-quality growth, modernization, & competitiveness. The 2022

National Social Science Fund of China.

Central Document No. 1 and the Government Work Report explicitly stated the need to vigorously promote the deep integration of new-generation information and digital technologies with agricultural production and management, accelerate the development of the digital economy, advance smart agriculture and digital countryside construction, and expand the application scenarios of the digital economy in agriculture and rural areas [2].

Existing research on the relationship between the digital economy and high-quality agricultural development primarily focuses on three angles: Firstly, the role of the digital economy in promoting agricultural digital transformation. Guo Suyu (2021) found that digital finance plays a pivotal role in advancing high-quality agricultural development [3]. Secondly, the optimization effect of the digital economy on agricultural production efficiency and resource allocation. Yao Yuchun and Li Bing (2023) discovered that the digital economy significantly enhances agricultural production by facilitating information flow, improving machinery and equipment, and enabling precise fertilization, thereby exerting information, equipment, and ecological effects [4].Thirdly, the pathways and mechanisms for the digital economy to promote high-quality agricultural development. Lu Zhangyang and Du Yutong (2022) found that the transformation and upgrading of industrial structures are crucial for the digital economy to empower high-quality agricultural development [5].

2   Research and Analysis on the Relationship Between Digital Economy and High-Quality Development of Agriculture

2.1   Analysis of the Direct Impact of Digital Economy on the High-Quality Development of Agriculture

The development of human capital is the cornerstone of high-quality rural development. Every stage of the manufacturing process, from field production methods to market terminal sales, technological advancements, and equipment upgrading, is heavily dependent on the experience and diligence of rural labor. Nonetheless, many young and middle-aged rural laborers opt to work outside of their hometowns due to the uneven overall economic growth level in China, which exacerbates the problem of a shortage of human capital in rural areas. The pace of agricultural modernization is slowed down or even stops as a result, further restricting the rise in the income levels of rural populations. This also weakens supply chain management, market supply capabilities, and agricultural production.

Through its distinct advantages and technological means, the digital economy directly affects a number of agricultural production issues, greatly increasing agricultural production efficiency, optimizing resource allocation, and encouraging the industry's overall modernization. For example, the use of sophisticated machinery like drones and smart agricultural machinery not only lowers the labor intensity of farmers but also greatly increases operational precision and efficiency. A scientific foundation for agricultural production is provided by the use of technologies like satellite remote sensing and meteorological data, which allow for more precise and real-time monitoring of crop growth environments and ultimately improve crop yields and quality.

The agricultural industrial chain is growing as a result of the extensive use of digital technology in agriculture, which is also creating new industrial forms and business models. For instance, the rise of live streaming and agricultural e-commerce has expanded the market for agricultural products by offering more practical and effective channels for sales of agricultural products. Furthermore, the digital economy fosters the integration of agriculture with tourism, culture, and other sectors of the economy, so unleashing the multifaceted potential of agriculture and reviving its superior development. Drawing from the theoretical study presented above, the following hypothesis is put forth:

H1: The development level of the digital economy can positively promote high-quality agricultural development.

2.2 Analysis on the Indirect Influence of Digital Economy on the High-Quality Development of Agriculture

The digital economy has developed at a rapid pace in recent years, resulting in significant changes. The first shift that stands out is the improvement of innovative skills and the optimization of human resources. The extensive use of digital technologies has increased the intelligence and customization of human resource management [6]. Thus, we cannot ignore the importance of agricultural skill development as a critical intermediary variable when examining how the digital economy affects high-quality agricultural development.

The digital economy requires agricultural workers with more comprehensive traits and innovative capabilities, while traditional models of talent development for the agriculture industry frequently concentrated on teaching theoretical knowledge and fundamental skills. The development of agricultural talent must therefore keep up with the times, placing a strong emphasis on the development of digital thinking, information technology skills, and market acumen. The growth of agricultural talent is closely linked to the digital economy through many channels such as industry-academia-research integration, university-business partnership, and others. This results in a group of highly skilled individuals who are adept in both digital and agricultural technology.

High-quality agricultural development is further propelled forward by the modernization and transformation of agricultural talent development. Increases in both the amount and quality of agricultural talent have had a substantial positive impact on market competitiveness, product quality, and agricultural production efficiency. Moreover, agricultural experts can apply optimal decision-making and refined management through digital technology in agricultural production processes, increasing environmental protection and resource utilization efficiency. Furthermore, they actively contribute to the advancement of agricultural science and technology, bringing fresh energy and vitality to the development of superior agriculture.

Therefore, through its strong enabling effect, the digital economy not only directly affects market mechanisms and agricultural production processes, but it also indirectly fosters the transformation and upgrading of agricultural talent development, providing a strong talent base for high-quality agricultural development. Drawing from the theoretical study presented above, the following conjecture is put forth:

H2: The digital economy can facilitate high-quality agricultural development by promoting the growth of agricultural talent development.

3   Empirical Analysis

3.1   Variable Selection

Calculation of Agricultural High Quality Level Index

Based on the overall requirements of high-quality development of China's economy in the new era and the profound consideration made by the particularity of the agricultural field, as well as the concept of high-quality development of China's economy in the new era, the comprehensive evaluation index system of high-quality development of agriculture is built from five aspects: innovation, coordination, green, opening, and sharing [10]. This option not only aligns with the macro orientation of the national development strategy, but it also accurately captures the internal demand and future development trend of agricultural transformation and upgrading.

In agriculture, technological innovation is critical for increasing productivity, optimizing structures, and improving competitiveness. New varieties, technology, and equipment improve agricultural intelligence and precision, propelling the sector to greater value. Innovation is the fundamental driving force behind high-quality agricultural development, propelling scientific and technological improvements. In the face of resource and environmental limits, green development is critical to long-term sustainability. A green indicator system guides low-carbon, circular agriculture while eliminating chemicals, saving the environment, and improving product quality and safety.

Agricultural high-quality development emphasizes collaborative and balanced development. A coordinated development indicator system examines the relationship between agriculture, the rural economy, the environment, and social development. An openness indicator system focusing on trade, investment, and technological collaboration measures the irreversible nature of agricultural cooperation under globalization. This improves China's agricultural competitiveness, broadens the growth scope, and optimizes resource allocation. An inclusivity indicator system reflects agricultural benefits for everybody, including farmer income, rural services, and urban-rural integration, so reducing the urban-rural divide, improving livelihoods, and sharing development gains.

As a result, this study proposes an agricultural high-quality development indicator system based on five core first-level indicators: innovation, green development, coordination, openness, and inclusiveness. By referring to Yang Junge's (2023) [8] definition of the connotation of agricultural high-quality development based on the new development concept and drawing on the evaluation index systems for economic high-quality development by Chen Menggen et al. (2020) [9], agricultural high-quality development by Liu Tao and Du Simeng (2021) [10], and Yu Ting and Yu Fawen (2021) [11], this paper conducts a comprehensive evaluation of high-quality development to more accurately The specific contents are outlined in the following table. In selecting the method for determining index weights, comprehensive consideration is given to the applicability of panel data, the objectivity of weight calculation, and ensuring the comparability of calculation results. Ultimately, the entropy weight-TOPSIS method is adopted to calculate the level of high-quality development. For reasons of space, only some of the tables are shown (Table 1).

Digital Economic Index Measurement

According to the specific content of the statistical classification, the National Bureau

Table 1. The index system of evaluation of high-quality agricultural development

Primary index	Secondary index	Three-level index	attribute
innovative development	Innovation foundation	Agricultural industrial structure adjustment index	forward direction
		Income distribution gap of rural residents	forward direction
		Urban and rural consumption level ratio	forward direction
		Income ratio between urban and rural residents	forward direction
	Innovation benefits	The importance of rural residents to health care	forward direction
		Rural residents have a rich life	forward direction
		The overall level of rural residents	forward direction
		Income level of rural residents	forward direction
green development	resource consumption	Agricultural products import and export dependence	negative direction
		Agricultural products market turnover proportion	negative direction
		Number of agricultural products markets	negative direction
		The proportion of foreign direct investment in agricultural investment	negative direction
	environmental pollution	The proportion of agricultural fixed asset investment	negative direction
		Rural land transfer rate	negative direction
		land area covered with trees	negative direction
	environmental protection	The amount of pesticides used per unit area	forward direction
Open development	resource optimization	Amount of chemical fertilizer applied per unit area	forward direction
		Use strength of agricultural plastic film	forward direction
		Energy consumption per unit of added value of agriculture, forestry, animal husbandry and fishery	forward direction
	Market optimization	Per capita electricity consumption of employees in the primary industry	forward direction
		Unit output value of agriculture, forestry, animal husbandry and fishery intermediate consumption	forward direction
		Ten thousand yuan of agricultural added value of water consumption	forward direction
Shared development	Living standards have improved	Number of green food products	forward direction
		Number of green food enterprises	negative direction

(continued)

Table 1. (*continued*)

Primary index	Secondary index	Three-level index	attribute
		land productivity	forward direction
		productivity of labour	forward direction
	Benefit sharing	Professional and technical number of agricultural economic institutions	negative direction
		Number of agricultural and economic institutions at the township level	negative direction
		The proportion of agricultural financial input	negative direction
harmonious development	Industrial coordination	level of farming mechanization	forward direction
	Urban and rural coordination	Binary contrast coefficient	forward direction

of Statistics will classify digital economy, digital industrialization and digital industry, and refer to Yang Huimei and Jiang Lu (2021) [12] define the digital economy and analysis and combined with chuan-hui liu and zhi-peng Yang (2021) [13] of digital economy development level index design, build urban agglomeration digital economy development index system, finally also use the entropy method for digital economy development level (Table 2).

Intermediary Variable Selection

It is acknowledged that, in choosing intermediary variables, agricultural practitioners must become more proficient in digital technologies in order to meet the demands of the market and adjust to new production techniques spurred by the digital economy. Concurrently, the growth of the digital economy has drawn more skilled workers to the agricultural industry, creating a large talent pool for the high-quality development of the agricultural sector. Thus, the intermediate variable chosen is the cultivation of agricultural talent. The quantity of graduates from agro technical training programs serves as a proxy for agricultural talent cultivation (*edu*).

Control Variable Selection

Drawing upon existing research findings [14, 15], the following variables are controlled: Rural ecological environment (*env*) can be represented by the affected area of crops due to disasters.Government support for agriculture (*Gsa*) can be indicated by fiscal expenditures on agriculture, forestry, and water affairs.Urbanization (*urb*) can be expressed as the ratio of the urban population to the total population.

3.2   Data Sources and Processing

Based on the previously indicated indicator system, data from 2012 to 2021 were chosen for the analysis. The China Statistical Yearbook, China Rural Statistical Yearbook, China Green Food Statistical Yearbook, China Rural Management and Operation Annual Report, China Commodity Trading Market Statistical Yearbook, China Energy Statistical Yearbook, and China Water Resources Bulletin were among the main sources of

Table 2. Digital economy development index system

Primary index	Secondary index	Three-level index	attribute
The development level of the digital economy	infrastructure	Optical cable line density (km/km 2)	forward direction
		Internet access port density (ports/person)	forward direction
		Number of websites per 100 enterprises (units)	forward direction
	Industrial scale	Average number of employees in the computer communications and other electronic equipment manufacturing industry (in ten thousand)	forward direction
		Main business revenue of the computer communications and other electronic equipment manufacturing industry (in billions of yuan)	forward direction
		Software business revenue (in billions of yuan)	forward direction
		Average number of employees in the software and information technology services industry (in ten thousand)	forward direction
	Life application	Mobile phone penetration rate (units per 100 people)	forward direction
		Average number of broadband Internet access subscriptions per person (subscriptions per person)	forward direction
		Internet penetration rate (%)	forward direction

(*continued*)

Table 2. (*continued*)

Primary index	Secondary index	Three-level index	attribute
	Production application	The Digital Financial Inclusion Index	forward direction
		E-commerce sales (in billions of yuan)	forward direction
		The percentage of enterprises engaged in e-commerce transactions out of the total number of enterprises (%)	forward direction
		Number of computers per 100 employees in enterprises (units)	forward direction

the pertinent data. The availability and completeness of the data were taken into careful account when building the indicator system. The variables utilized had little to no missing data, and interpolation techniques were used to fill in the blanks for those variables that had missing values in specific years, guaranteeing the consistency and fullness of the data.

3.3 Model Specification

The two-way fixed effects model refers to a panel data model that controls for both time and regional fixed effects, effectively accounting for individual characteristics that do not vary over time and temporal features that remain constant across regions. To investigate the influence of digital economy on the high-quality development of agriculture, the model is formulated as Eq. (1), where t represents the city, i denotes the year, $Aqua_{it}$ signifies the level of high-quality agricultural development, Dig_{it} represents the level of digital economy development, and β measures the degree of impact that digital economy has on the high-quality development of agriculture. Additionally, x_{it} stands for a series of control variables, while δ_t and u_i are included to represent the year fixed effects and city fixed effects, respectively. Lastly, ε_{it} represents the random disturbance term.

$$Aqua_{it} = \alpha + \beta Dig_{it} + \gamma x_{it} + u_i + \delta_t + \varepsilon_{it} \tag{1}$$

To further explore the path through which digital economy influences the high-quality development of agriculture, we draw upon the mediation model design approach proposed by Wen Zhonglin (2004) [16] and construct a mediation effect model as follows. Here, denotes the mediating variable, which is agricultural talent cultivation. Equation (2) examines the relationship between digital economy and the mediating variable, while Eq. (3) investigates the relationship between the mediating variable and the high-quality development level of agriculture. Additionally, Sobel test and Bootstrap test are employed to enhance the robustness of the mediation effect.

$$edu_{it} = \alpha + \beta_1 Dig_{it} + \gamma x_{it} + u_i + \delta_t + \varepsilon_{it} \tag{2}$$

$$Aqua_{it} = \alpha + \beta_2 Dig_{it} + \beta_3 edu_{it} + \gamma x_{it} + u_i + \delta_t + \varepsilon_{it} \tag{3}$$

3.4 Benchmark Regression

To avoid potential multicollinearity issues, the variance inflation factor (VIF) among variables was calculated, and it was found that all variables were within 10, indicating no multicollinearity problem. The Hausman test revealed a P-value of 0.0000, implying that the estimation results of the fixed effects model are superior to those of the random effects model, so the fixed effects model was applied for empirical testing, and the results are presented in Table 3.

Table 3. Benchmark Regression Results Table

variable	Aqua			
	(1)	(2)	(3)	(4)
dig	0.6611***	0.2559***	0.4150***	0.2189***
	(15.39)	(5.88)	(8.01)	(4.65)

Note: ***, ** and * indicate significance at the 1%, 5%, and 10% levels, respectively; t-values are in parentheses.

According to the findings, the Digital Economy Index (Dig) coefficient is positive and significant, implying that the advancement of the digital economy has a favorable impact on the high-quality growth of agriculture. This might be linked to the digital economy's introduction of modern information technology and intelligent instruments, which considerably improve the intelligence and precision of agricultural production, promoting green and sustainable agricultural development. The positive correlation between urbanization and high-quality agricultural development (p-value < 0.05) suggests that as urbanization progresses, a significant number of rural laborers relocate to cities. This helps to decrease the overstock of conventional rural labor. Agriculture output becomes more intensive and efficient as a result of this well-organized labor flow, which also optimizes the structure of agricultural labor. Furthermore, government assistance for agriculture is favorably connected with high-quality agricultural development. The government directly supports farmers with financial help by enacting more fiscal measures in this regard. The creation of agricultural infrastructure, the advancement of agricultural technology, promotion, and the prevention and relief of agricultural disasters are just a few of the uses for these monies, all of which are crucial protections for the growth of superior agriculture.

A higher number of crop disaster-affected areas (i.e., deterioration of the ecological environment or an increase in unfavorable natural conditions) would have a negative impact on high-quality agricultural development, given that the variable chosen for the rural ecological environment is the crop disaster-affected area and the negative correlation between high-quality agricultural development and crop disaster-affected area.

3.5 Endogeneity Test

We have consulted pertinent literature for assistance because there is a chance that unidentified endogeneity links among variables exist and could cause regression biases. As an instrumental variable for the digital economy index, we first used the methodology of Huang Qunhui et al. (2019) by using the historical postal and telecommunications data of each city in 1984 [20]. Additionally, we multiplied the total postal and telecom business volume of each province in 1984 by the telephone penetration rate of each city in the year prior, in accordance with Nunn and Qian's (2014) methodology. We then used this interaction term as the instrumental variable for the provincial digital economy index in that year [21]. In addition, we performed the endogeneity test using the Generalized Method of Moments estimator (GMM2S). After taking into account temporal and cross-sectoral heterogeneities, the GMM2S approach can handle endogeneity with effectiveness and yield reliable and efficient estimates of model parameters.

Table 4. Endogeneity test results table

variable	Primary index	Secondary index
dig		0.3907***
		(2.0019)
iv	0.0016***	
	(4.1151)	
R-squared	0.6260	0.678

The results of our endogeneity test utilizing the GMM2S approach are displayed in Table 4. The digital economy index and instrumental variables have a strong association, and the coefficient of the digital economy is still significant at the 0.01 level. Additionally, we reject the tests for weak instrumental variables and insufficient instrumental variable identification, suggesting that the instrumental variable selection process is successful. The aforementioned findings suggest that the digital economy continues to significantly support the high-quality growth of agriculture even when endogeneity concerns are taken into account.

3.6 Mediation Effect Test

The purpose of the mediation effect test is to ascertain if one or more mediating variables convey the influence of an independent variable on a dependent variable. The cultivation of agricultural skill was chosen as the mediating variable for our evaluation in this paper. The estimated coefficient of the digital economy on technical innovation is highly positive, as shown by the data in the following table. This suggests that the digital economy positively drives technological innovation. Additionally, as shown in column (2), there is a significant positive estimate of the digital economy's coefficient on the development of high-quality agriculture. With a value of 0.1781, which is less than the anticipated coefficient of 0.2189 in the benchmark regression column (3), the impact coefficient of agricultural talent nurturing on high-quality development in column (2) is likewise significantly positive. This indicates that, with a mediation impact accounting for 22.91% of the total effect, agricultural talent cultivation functions as a mediating variable in the digital economy's promotion of high-quality agricultural development. These results lead us to the conclusion that Hypothesis 2 is validated (Table 5).

Table 5. Of intermediary test results

	(1)	(2)	(3)
	edu	Aqua	Aqua
dig	9.1967***	0.1781***	0..2189***
	(6.45)	(3.44)	(4.65)
edu		0.0041*	
		(1.93)	
adj. R^2	0.4733	0.7666	0.7679

3.7 Heterogeneity Test

Due to its large size and varied and complicated geographic locations, China has a major disparity in resources, which in turn causes notable imbalances in regional economies and capacities for innovation. According to Liu Wei (2024), the samples were split into two main regions: the south and the north, with the Qinling Mountains and Huaihe River acting as the division. This was done in order to account for the effects of various geographic locations on grain ecological efficiency (Table 6).

Table 6. Provincial division table

area	province
South	Jiangsu, Zhejiang, Anhui, Shanghai, Fujian, Jiangxi, Hubei, Hunan, Guangdong, Guangxi, Hainan, Sichuan, Chongqing, Guizhou, Yunnan
North	Beijing, Tianjin, Hebei, Liaoning, Shanxi, Inner Mongolia, Jilin, Heilongjiang, Shandong, Henan, Shaanxi, Gansu, Qinghai, Ningxia, Xinjiang

As can be seen in the above table, the regression coefficient between the digital economy and agricultural high-quality development in the northern region is 0.4272, which is significantly positively correlated at the 1% level. This suggests that the digital economy significantly contributes to the development of agricultural high-quality development in the northern region. Although the regression coefficient between the digital economy and agricultural high-quality development in the southern region is positive (0.1013), it does not reach statistical significance, indicating that the driving force behind the development of agricultural high-quality development in the southern region is not as great as it is in the northern region (Table 7).

Table 7. Provincial division table

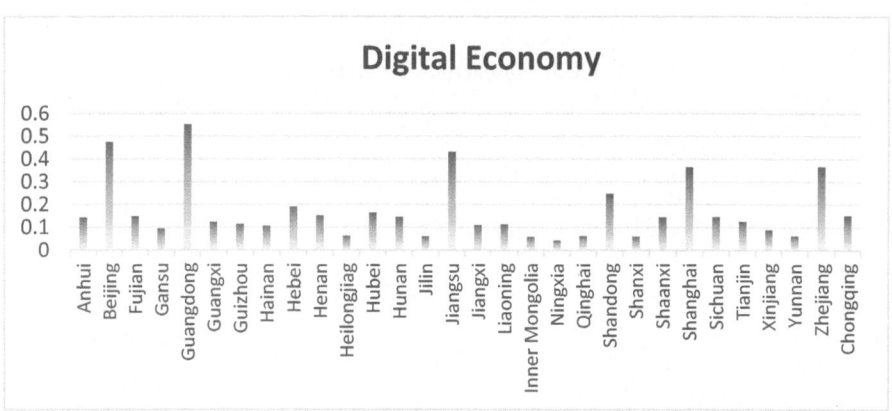

The total digital economy in China's southern agricultural main production regions is higher than that of the country's northern agricultural main production areas, according to our calculations of the digital economies of each province. We therefore deduce that one plausible explanation could be that the southern areas have emerged as leaders in the digital economy's development and have attained a cutting-edge degree of digitization, with a broad and profound penetration into the agriculture sector. Due to this advantage, southern agriculture is able to reap the benefits of digital transformation sooner. These benefits include increased production efficiency, instant access to market information, and more accurate allocation of agricultural resources. As a result, the marginal effect of the digital economy on the advancement of high-quality agricultural development is somewhat diminished, as evidenced by the correlation regression coefficient's insignificance.

On the other hand, the agricultural system in the northern region generally adheres to the conventional paradigm, and the region started late in the digital economy. In light of this, the introduction and use of green digital technologies has emerged as a major force behind northern agricultural reform, helping to improve productivity, optimize resource allocation, significantly lessen environmental impact, and hasten the transition of agriculture into high-quality development. The promotion of the high-quality development of northern agriculture is thus significantly aided by the digital economy, and statistical regression analysis also reveals a high degree of significance for its coefficient.

We endeavor to delve further into the particular causes of the disparities between the north and the south, but this calls for in-depth research and the creation of models that correlate to the disparities in the regional infrastructure, policies, and economic circumstances between the north and the south. The available information is insufficient to fully support this claim; additional study or supporting data may be required in the future (Table 8).

Table 8. Heterogeneity Test Results Table

	South	North
Dig	0.1013	0.4272^{***}
	(1.52)	(5.32)
adj. R2	0.8050	0.7669

4 Conclusions and Suggestions

4.1 Conclusions

Based on panel data from 2012 to 2021 from 30 Chinese provinces, regions, and municipalities, the study empirically investigates the relationship and mechanism between the degree of digital economy development and high-quality agriculture development. The empirical findings indicate that: First, in 30 Chinese provinces, the digital economy can support the growth of high-quality agriculture. Second, the growth of the digital economy has drawn more skilled individuals to the agricultural sector, offering a solid talent guarantee for the industry's superior development. Third, the influence of the digital economy on the development of high-quality agriculture varies depending on the region. The northern region benefits greatly from the digital economy, whereas the southern region does not benefit as much as the northern region does from high-quality agricultural growth.

4.2 Suggestions

Strengthening Digital Economy's Empowerment of Agriculture Strategies to Promote High-Quality Agricultural Development Nationwide
In 30 provinces, autonomous regions, and municipalities throughout the nation, the digital economy—as a new engine for China's economic development—has significantly contributed to the development of high-quality agriculture. Consequently, the government has to fortify the development of infrastructure, augment funding for infrastructure like broadband networks, mobile Internet, and Internet of things in rural regions, and guarantee the extensive integration of digital economy in the agricultural domain. It is important to prioritize network coverage, particularly in rural and underdeveloped

areas. Second, in order to achieve the interconnection and sharing of agricultural production, processing, sales, and other links of data, we should also create and enhance the agricultural data platform system. It offers a scientific foundation for agricultural production decisions and market forecasts through data mining and analysis. Encouraging the development of agricultural branding is another effective way to bolster the branding of agricultural products through digital economic means. By using social media, e-commerce platforms, and other channels, high-quality agricultural product brands can be promoted. This would increase the agricultural products' market influence and brand value and help the country's agriculture attain high-quality development.

Optimizing Talent Recruitment and Cultivation Mechanisms to Facilitate the Digital Transformation of Agriculture

Empirical research has led to the understanding that the development of agricultural talent acts as a mediating factor in the process by which the digital economy fosters the development of superior agriculture. On the one hand, the digital economy improves agricultural talent development quality by offering a wealth of educational resources and cutting edge teaching techniques. Conversely, high-quality agricultural development can be fueled by the results of cultivating agricultural talent since they can be immediately applied to agricultural production methods. In conclusion, the development of agricultural talent is a crucial mediating factor that propels the agricultural modernization movement driven by the digital economy.

For this reason, we suggest a "Digital Agriculture Talent Introduction Program" that is suited to the industry's requirements for digital transformation. This entails developing strategies to draw in specialists in data analysis, IT, and agri-economic management. Providing career pathways, financing for research, and entrepreneurial support will create a diverse pool of people that combines digital and agri-expertise. To improve the literacy and application skills of rural youth, returnees, and current farmers, we also need to step up our training programs for digital skills. Modern digital technology and concepts are integrated into agri-education through a school-enterprise, industry-education paradigm, which revitalizes the industry and develops practical skills for high-quality development.

Strengthening Differentiated Policy Support and Precisely Targeting Market Demands

Policies should be tailored to local circumstances and each area's unique characteristics should be thoroughly researched in order to overcome regional disparities. The government ought to assemble expert teams to carry out thorough assessments of the Northern and Southern areas' respective strengths and shortcomings in terms of agricultural resources, infrastructure, farmer digital literacy, and market demands. In order to guarantee that policies are closely in line with the real conditions on the ground, specific plans for the digital economic development of both regions should be developed based on the findings of these surveys.

Given that the Northern region's digital economy is still in its infancy, the government ought to invest more in order to hasten the development of new infrastructure, including big data centers, 5G, and the Internet of Things (IoT), which will greatly aid in the digital transformation of agriculture. On the other hand, the Southern area ought to prioritize the advancement of technologies in the field of digital agriculture. In order to promote high-quality agricultural development through innovation, the Southern area should be encouraged to take advantage of its current advantages in digital technology to investigate more varied agricultural applications, such as smart agriculture and precision farming.

References

1. Zhiheng, J.: Spatial differences and driving mechanisms of high-quality agricultural and rural development in China. J. Quant. Tech. Econ. **12**, 25–44 (2021)
2. Zhou, Q., Li, X.: Digital economy and high-quality agricultural development: internal mechanisms and empirical analysis. Reform Econ. Syst. (06), 82–89 (2022)
3. Guo, S.: Strategies for digital finance to empower high-quality agricultural development. Price Theory Pract. (12), 102–105 (2021)
4. Yao, Y., Li, B.: Digital economy empowering high-quality agricultural development: mechanism analysis and empirical test. J. Southeast Univ. (Philos. Soc. Sci. Ed.) **25**(05): 53–63+147 (2023)
5. Zhangyang, L., Yutong, D.: An empirical study on the digital economy empowering high-quality agricultural development. China Bus. Market **36**(11), 3–14 (2022)
6. Yanfei, W.: Research on the innovative development of enterprise human resource management mode in the digital economy era. Enterp. Reform Manage. **06**, 102–104 (2024). https://doi.org/10.13768/j.cnki.cn11-3793/f.2024.0331
7. Zhongyu, L., Wakasi, R.: Regional differences and dynamic evolution of high-quality agricultural development in China. J. Quant. Tech. Econ. **38**(06), 28–44 (2021). https://doi.org/10.13653/j.cnki.jqte.2021.06.002
8. Junge, Y., Qinmei, W.: Digital technology and high-quality agricultural development: from the perspective of digital productivity. J. Shanxi Univ. Financ. Econ. **45**(04), 47–63 (2023). https://doi.org/10.13781/j.cnki.1007-9556.2023.04.004
9. Chen Menggen, X., Ying, Z.Y.: Statistical evaluation and regional comparison of high-quality economic development under the new development concept: based on an improved TOPSIS comprehensive evaluation model. J. Stat. Sci. Pract. **1**(2), 1–14 (2020)
10. Tao, L., Simeng, D.: Construction of evaluation index system for high-quality agricultural development based on the new development concept. Chin. J. Agric. Resour. Reg. Plann. **42**(4), 1–9 (2021)
11. Ting, Y., Fawen, Y.: Evaluation of high-quality agricultural development and obstacle factor diagnosis based on entropy weight TOPSIS method. Yunnan Soc. Sci. **5**, 76–83 (2021)
12. Huimei, Y., Jiang, L.: Digital economy, spatial effects, and total factor productivity. Stat. Res. **38**(04), 3–15 (2021). https://doi.org/10.19343/j.cnki.11-1302/c.2021.04.001
13. Chuanhui, L., Zhipeng, Y.: Measurement of urban agglomeration digital economy index and analysis of spatiotemporal differences: a case study of six major urban agglomerations. Mod. Manage. Sci. **04**, 92–111 (2021)
14. Yiding, H., Xiaoyu, D., Jingwei, Y.: Research on the impact of digital economy on the high-quality development of Chinese agriculture. Shanxi Rural Econ. **12**, 46–48 (2024). https://doi.org/10.16675/j.cnki.cn14-1065/f.2024.12.015
15. Li, Z., Ma, L., Wang, Y.: Theoretical logic and empirical test of digital economy empowering high-quality agricultural development. Bus. Econ. (07), 27–31+47 (2024). https://doi.org/10.19905/j.cnki.syjj1982.2024.07.020
16. Zhonglin, W., Lei, Z., Jietai, H.: Mediation effect test procedure and its application. Acta Psychol. Sin. **05**, 614–620 (2004)
17. Huang, Q., Sheng, F.: The new quality productivity system: element characteristics, structural support, and functional orientation. Reform (2), 15–24 (2024).
18. Nunn, N, Qian, N.: US food aid and civil conflict. Am. Econ. Rev. **104**(6), 1630–1666 (2014)

Application and Industry Track

Empirical Study on User Acceptance and Optimization Strategies of AIGC News

Chenduan[✉], Yechensang[✉], and Xiazhen

School of Culture and Media, Central University of Finance and Economics, Beijing 100083, China

anna_chenduan@163.com, 201906050630@zjut.edu.cn

Abstract. In today's digital era, the rapid development of intelligent media, constantly squeezing the survival space of traditional media. The wide application of Internet technology and digital technology in the news industry has subverted the traditional news dissemination mode, and the identity of news readers has completed the metamorphosis from the passive "audience" to the active choice of "users". This study focuses on the user acceptance of AIGC news, not only studying the overall user acceptance of AIGC news, but also trying to analyse the impact of users' demographically characteristics on the acceptance of AIGC news. At the same time, this study also explores the expectations and concerns of users for AIGC news, considers the advantages and shortcomings of current AIGC news, and tries to propose targeted optimization strategies. Based on the relevant theories of previous scholars and the current situation of AIGC news, this study designed a questionnaire and used SPSS software to collate and analyse the data. It is found that the overall acceptance of AIGC news is high, and the overall acceptance of AIGC news is little affected by demographic factors; in addition, users are concerned about the authenticity of AIGC news, which is affected by copyright factors; and the preference of AIGC news types shows significant differences. Finally, this study also tries to propose optimization strategies for the problems of AIGC news from the perspectives of enhancing the credibility of AIGC news, optimizing the user experience of AIGC news and strengthening the copyright protection of AIGC news.

Keywords: AIGC · User Acceptance · Optimization Strategies

1 Introduction

On 30th November 2022, OpenAI's large-scale language generation model ChatGPT was launched, and AIGC came into the public's view and life. Along with the rapid development and accumulation of AI technology, AIGC technology is gradually becoming mature, and is more commonly used in a wide range of fields [1]. AIGC technology has a broad application prospect. The wind of AI technology is also rapidly blowing to the media industry. In recent years, more and more media have introduced AI technology in the production, dissemination and feedback of news products. The in-depth integration of AI technology in the news production process has become an important way to further

C. Xing et al. (Eds.): METAVERSE 2024, LNCS 15429, pp. 51–67, 2025.
https://doi.org/10.1007/978-3-031-76977-1_4

deepen the transformation of intelligent media. AIGC technology is a new revolution for the media industry [2].

This paper aims to study the user acceptance and optimization strategy of AIGC news. Combined with the existing relevant theories and practices, it analyses the users' expectations and concerns about AIGC news, and puts forward targeted countermeasures and suggestions from different dimensions, so as to provide reference for accelerating the transformation of intelligent media.

The study aims to investigate user acceptance of Artificial Intelligence Generated Content (AIGC) news. It seeks to understand not only the overall acceptance but also how demographic characteristics influence this acceptance. Additionally, it explores user expectations and concerns regarding AIGC news and proposes optimization strategies based on the findings.

Key research questions of the paper includes:
What is the overall user acceptance of AIGC news?
How do demographic factors affect the acceptance of AIGC news?
What are the user expectations and concerns regarding AIGC news?
How can AIGC news be optimized to meet user expectations and address concerns?

The study considers demographic factors such as age, gender, education level, and occupation to understand their impact on the acceptance of AIGC news. Users express concerns about the authenticity of AIGC news, influenced by factors such as copyright issues. There is also variability in the preference for different types of AIGC news among users. Based on the findings, the study suggests strategies to enhance the credibility of AIGC news, optimize user experience, and strengthen copyright protection to address user concerns and improve the quality of AIGC news.

This paper adopts the method of empirical research to study the user acceptance and optimization of AIGC news. It is to understand the user acceptance of different types of AIGC news, summarize the expectations and concerns of users for AIGC news. The study also puts forward targeted countermeasures and suggestions in the light of the existing problems. On the one hand, it helps to promote the research progress of intelligent media transformation of financial media. On the other hand, the use of empirical research methods to analyse the user acceptance of the latest AI technology in the media news production process can help grasp the latest market trends and provide reference for more media.

2 Literature Review and Research Hypotheses

2.1 Conceptual Definition

AIGC (Generative Artificial Intelligence) is a new type of content creation method, which refers to the technology based on the technical methods of artificial intelligence such as generative adversarial networks and large models, and the technology of generating relevant content with appropriate generalization ability through learning and recognition of existing data [3]. It inherits the advantages of professionally produced content (PGC, Professional- generated Content) and user-generated content (UGC, User-generated Content), and gives full play to the advantages of AI technology to create a new form of digital content generation and interaction [4].

AIGC news refers to the introduction of AI technology into the news production process, assisting journalists in news writing, video generation, data analysis and so on. With the help of AI technology, the news production process of gathering, writing, editing and commenting can save a lot of cost and time for the media, improve production efficiency and create higher revenue. AIGC technology has impacted the production relations of news production, enabling news organisations to automate the generation of news articles. AIGC generates news stories quickly by using natural language processing algorithms to analyse and summarise large amounts of data. Generative AI has revolutionised media production methods and means of communication, allowing different types of text, pictures and videos to be converted into each other, breaking down the boundaries of media forms, enriching the form of reporting, and enhancing the effectiveness of communication.

User acceptance refers to the acceptance of a new product or a feature by users. This concept is derived from the User Acceptance Test and the Technology Acceptance Model. According to the Technology Acceptance Model (TAM) and its extension (TAM/TAM2), perceived ease of use and perceived usefulness influence user acceptance behavior [5]. The Unified Theory of Acceptance and Use of Technology (UTAUT) focuses on the influence of variables such as performance expectations, effort expectations, social influence, and convenience on user acceptance, which are also influenced by demographically characteristics such as gender, age, and experience [6]. User acceptance is mainly applied in the study of information technology user acceptance, while AIGC news is a convergence product that integrates AIGC technology with news production process, which is also applicable to the study of information technology user acceptance.

2.2 Impact of AIGC Technology on the News Production Process

Through the combing of related literature, it can be found that there is a rich research on the change of AIGC technology on the traditional news production process, and these researches mainly think about the problem from the perspective of news producers. Researchers generally believe that AIGC technology has great potential for development in improving the production efficiency of news products. According to the World Association of News Publishers, personalized news, translation and whole-process efficiency improvement are currently the three most promising directions for integrating AI technology in the news production process. Diakopoulos (2023) summarizes the main functions of generative AI technology in the news production chain as three: (1) Generate and process text, such as assessing the newsworthiness of text, analyzing documents and classifying and tagging them, processing and translating raw data from multilingual text, creating different styles of tweets based on different social media, etc. (2) Edit and process visual information, such as editing multi-format photographs and videos, and generating charts and graphs based on content topics. (3) Optimizing algorithm-based workflows, e.g. Personalizing tweets for different audience segments, automatically reviewing and deleting inappropriate comments [7]. Konrad et al. suggest that if the knowledge industry wants to develop and innovate the application of AI technology in the future, the first thing to focus on is human-machine collaboration, rather than leaving all work tasks to AI robots [8].

China is a leading country in the world in terms of AI technology innovation and scene application. Domestic academics have conducted some profound discussions and cutting-edge explorations on the application and control of AI technology in the news production process. In researching and analyzing the interaction between workers and AI, scholars such as Xu Jing (2023) believe that in the future, the media should reasonably allocate the proportion of generative AI-assisted human work and generative AI automation work [9]. Chen and Cai (2022) argue that AI should be used to assist human work and automate work. They believe that AI technology is the core of the new generation of automation technology system, which can replace labour factors with capital factors and thus achieve the role of promoting growth.AI products can both replace and supplement the work of workers, that is, there are substitution and complementary effects between capital and labour factors. At the same time, the rapid development of AI technology can also create more job opportunities. In the new work plan, human beings have more advantages and cannot be replaced by AI robots [10]. In the field of news, Zhang and Zhou (2023) believe that the news media's application of AI technology covers a wide range of parts from content production, auditing to multimedia dissemination, etc., with prominent innovations such as AI writing, AI auditing, AI short-video generation and AI TV [8]. Artificial intelligence-generated content provides more data and tools, changing the way news is produced and accelerating the generation and dissemination of news stories, but at the same time raising a range of ethical, quality and cost-control challenges:

Authenticity: Hao Yu and Wen Xi (2023) believe that ChatGPT can only process and handle information, and the content generated by it is neither original nor verified [11]. And when AI's big model computing data produces data news, the three main technical elements of AI - big data, strong algorithms, and supercomputing power - are all elements that breed fake news. The reason for this is that AI-generated content often does not undergo the ethical scrutiny and fact-checking that traditional journalists do, damaging the reputation of the news industry. Even some political groups and special interest groups can use AIGC to create fake news and false comments.

Value Orientation: Zhang and Zhou (2023) pointed out that if the news production process is completely controlled by AI robots, the media may lose its original control over society and public opinion. The agenda-setting function of the media, i.e. the gatekeeper function of the media, will be gradually weakened and replaced by algorithms and AI [8]. AIGC news usually generates content based on data and facts; they lack subjective judgement and values. This can lead to news stories that lack position and in-depth analysis and simply present facts.

Cost: According to Zhang and Zhou (2023), although the introduction of AI technology into the media news production line can achieve full automation of news production, however, structuring raw data and constructing algorithmic models require a large number of professional media workers and technicians, which will incur a large amount of human resource costs. At the same time, in order to continuously produce AIGC news, a large amount of data is needed as a means of production, and the media, while enjoying the convenience of media intelligence, must also pay for the cost of data collection and use [8].

2.3   User Acceptance Study of AIGC News

It is not enough for AIGC News to have a strong technological superiority in the production process, but it is also necessary to win over more users in the process of diffusion of innovations. The theory of innovation and diffusion suggests that innovation refers to ideas, things or products that are regarded as novel by individuals or other adopting units, and the diffusion of innovation refers to the basic social process by which innovations are accepted by people. Although a large number of media are actively introducing AIGC technology into the news production process and producing AIGC news products, users are undoubtedly the most crucial factor in the diffusion of AIGC news as an innovative product. As consumers of news products, users' preferences and tendencies towards AIGC news will determine the development direction of AIGC news.

Sohn (2020) and other scholars used users' behavioural intentions towards AI products to model user acceptance, and the results of the study showed that users' acceptance of the products was influenced more by their interest in the technology than by utilitarian aspects [5]. Chopra examines the issue of user acceptance of AI products in developing countries and finds that Indian use of AI products is largely influenced by factors such as trust, experience, ease of use, instrumentality and creativity [12].

When confronted with AI technologies and related products, users' perspectives are generally complex and contradictory [13]. On the one hand, many users believe that AI can simplify operational procedures and improve efficiency [13]. On the other hand, many users also have antipathy towards AI, believing that real people are better able to understand their needs [13]. Scholars such as Tzu-Kwan Lin (2021) believe that current AI technology is far from mature, which is an important reason why users are reluctant to encounter AI in most services [14]. Castelo et al. (2019) argue that users' aversion to AI is not entirely due to the unsatisfactory performance of AI's technology, but rather the presence of some psychological barriers preventing them from using AI technology. Segmenting different populations, characteristics such as gender, age, and experience moderated users' exposure to AI technology behaviours [15].

Based on the relevant research results and practical experience described in the previous section, this article focuses on news works based on AIGC technology, and investigates what type of AIGC news is more acceptable to the public, as well as the public's concerns and expectations. The following hypotheses are proposed in this study:

H1: Overall user acceptance of AIGC news is high.
H2: Differences in acceptance of AIGC news among users with different demographic attributes.
H3: Users have concerns about the authenticity of AIGC news.
H4: Users have concerns about the copyright of AIGC news.
H5: Preferences for types of AIGC news vary among users with different demographic attributes.

3 Research Methodology and Design

This paper combines the research methods of literature research, questionnaire survey and statistical analysis. Through the library and the Internet and other channels, the team consulted a large number of AIGC-related research materials, studied AI technology, AIGC news and other related knowledge, and tried to find ideas for designing experiments.

This experiment used a quantitative research method to collect data through an online questionnaire. The questionnaire included basic demographic information (age, gender, education level, occupation) and preferences for various aspects of AIGC news (text, picture, video news) As well as evaluation of its efficiency, objectivity and personalized recommendations. The data were also analyzed using SPSS software and the main statistical indicators included mean, standard deviation, minimum, maximum, variance, skewness and kurtosis.

With an online survey to the users of AIGC News as the main research object and designed a set of user acceptance questionnaire, the team aims to analyzed the data obtained and get insight into the basic situation of AIGC news user acceptance.

The questionnaire is placed from March 15 to March 31, 2024, in an AIGC technology online community. A total of 122 questionnaires were collected, a total of 122 valid questionnaires,and the sample is comprised of 58 male users (47.54%) and 64 female user (52.46%),among which 29 sample users aged 18 and below (23.77%), 30 sample users aged 18–28 (24.59%), 27 sample users aged 28–38 (22.13%), and 36 sample users aged 38 and above (29.51%). As for educational characteristics, 33 sample users have high school education or below (27.05%),40 sample users have college/bachelor's degree (32.79%),and the last 44 sample users have master's degree or above (36.07%). According to their occupational characteristics, 43 sample work in tertiary industry, accounting for 35.25%; 34 are employees of enterprises, accounting for 27.89%; and 45 are freelancers, accounting for 36.89. Data Analysis and Results.

3.1 Descriptive Analysis

This experiment collects users' socio-demographic data, users' preferences for different types of AIGC news, and users' expectations and concerns about AIGC news. Through the analysis, it can be concluded that users generally approve of AIGC news, especially the performance of AIGC news in terms of efficiency and personalized recommendation (Table 1).

The results of the data analyses indicated that participants were more receptive to AIGC news overall, with mean ratings exceeding the median on all indicators. In particular, preference for AIGC text news (mean = 2.25, standard deviation = 1.132) was slightly higher than for video news (mean = 2.18, standard deviation = 1.227) and photo news (mean = 2.13, standard deviation = 1.185). In terms of efficiency and personalized recommendations, participants gave relatively high ratings (means = 2.29 and 2.20, respectively). Skewness and kurtosis analyses showed a relatively normal distribution of data with no significant spiking.

Table 1. Descriptive statistics

	N	Min	Max	Avg	SD	variance	skewness		kurtosis	
	statisticians	Statisticians	statisticians	statisticians	statisticians	statisticians	statisticians	standard error	statisticians	standard error
1. Your age is	122	2	5	3.57	1.149	1.321	−.067	.219	−1.428	.435
2. Your gender be	122	1	2	1.52	.501	.251	−.100	.219	−2.024	.435
3. Your maximum Educational attainment is	122	1	3	2.13	.813	.660	−.246	.219	−1.443	.435
4. Your occupation is (please select the most) (close one)	122	2	4	3.02	.853	.727	−.032	.219	−1.630	.435
6. For AIGC Level of preference for text-based news	122	1	5	2.25	1.132	1.282	.838	.219	.049	.435
7. For AIGC Degree of preference for photo journalism	122	1	5	2.13	1.185	1.404	.954	.219	.022	.435
8. For AIGC Degree of preference for video news	122	1	5	2.18	1.227	1.504	1.015	.219	.108	.435
12 AIGC News in Efficiency what way	122	1	5	2.29	1.189	1.413	.865	.219	−.077	.435

This study confirms the high level of user acceptance of AIGC news, with particular emphasis on positive ratings in terms of video news content, efficiency and personalized recommendations.

3.2 Data Reliability Studies

This study explores users' preference and acceptance of Artificial Intelligence Generated Content (AIGC) news on different dimensions (text, images, video, efficiency, objectivity, personalized recommendations, and overall acceptance) through a quantitative approach. The reliability of the questionnaire was assessed using the Cronbach's Alpha coefficient, which showed an overall reliability coefficient of .934, indicating that the questionnaire had a very high internal consistency. Statistical analysis of the 122 valid questionnaires revealed that this study revealed positive user ratings and high acceptance of AIGC news.

This study adopts a quantitative research method and collects data through an online survey format, with 122 questionnaires distributed, all of which are valid samples. The questionnaire contained seven questions evaluating various aspects of AIGC news, and the evaluation dimensions covered the degree of preference for text news, photo news, and video news, as well as the performance of AIGC news in terms of efficiency, objectivity, personalized recommendations, and overall acceptance. The data were analyzed for reliability using SPSS software to assess the internal consistency of the scales, and the Cronbach's alpha coefficient was used as the evaluation index.

The results of the analyses show that the overall Clonbach Alpha Coefficient is .934, indicating that the questionnaire has a high degree of reliability. The mean values of the indicators ranged from 2.13 to 2.34, and the standard deviations ranged from 1.113 to 1.227, reflecting a relatively consistent and positive evaluation of all aspects of AIGC news by users. The Cronbach alpha coefficient after deleting any item changed slightly, but remained above .920, further demonstrating the stability and reliability of the scale. In addition, the corrected item-to-total correlations ranged from .746 to .832, demonstrating a high degree of correlation between individual items and overall ratings.

This study confirms the high acceptance and positive evaluation of AIGC news by users, and the scale demonstrates excellent reliability and consistency. The results indicate that users generally perceive AIGC News as efficient, objective and capable of meeting individual needs in providing news content.

3.3 Data Validity Assessment

This study used KMO and Bartlett's test of sphericity to assess the structural validity of this AIGC News User Acceptance Questionnaire. The KMO test was used to measure the degree of partial correlation between the variables to see if they were suitable for factor analysis, while the Bartlett's test was used to assess whether the observed variables were independent of each other in the aggregate. The analysis showed that the KMO sampling suitability measure was .925 and the significance of the Bartlett's test of sphericity was .000, indicating that the data were well suited for factor analysis, and the results showed a high degree of inter-correlation among the items of the questionnaire, which suggests that the scale has reliability and applicability in terms of validity.

4   Results

4.1   T-test Analysis

This study examines the effect of gender factor on the overall acceptance of AIGC news. The author first did an independent sample test on 122 users, and the data showed that there was no significant difference between males (n = 58) and females (n = 64) in the overall acceptance of AIGC news (t(120) = −.527, p = .599). The experiment shows that the gender factor does not constitute a significant influence in the overall acceptance of AIGC news.

4.2   Relevance Analysis

In this study, a correlation analysis was done on the data of 122 users in an attempt to explore the correlation between the sociolect-demographic variables of the users on the overall acceptance of AIGC news.

The results of the analyses show that the correlation coefficients between age, gender, highest level of education, and occupation and overall acceptance of AIGC news are −.009, .048, −.046, and .100, respectively, with corresponding two-tailed significant p-values of .920, .599, .617, and .274, respectively, which suggests that there is no statistically significant correlation between these variables and the overall acceptance of AIGC news. Significant correlation. This finding suggests that factors other than these basic socio-demographic variables may need to be explored for the development and optimisation of AIGC news content (Table 2).

Table 2. Relevance

relevance		1. Your age is		2. Your gender is	3. Your Highest level of education is	4. Your occupation is	15. Your overall acceptance of AIGC news is as follows Ho:
1. Your age is	Pearson correlation	1		.018	−.046	.016	−.009
	Significant (bobtail)			.841	.616	.864	.920
	Number of cases	122		122	122	122	122
2. Your gender is	Horatio Pearson (1758–1805), British mathematician correlate	.018		1	−.109	−.020	.048
	Significant (bobtail)	.841			.230	.825	.599
	Number of cases	122		122	122	122	122
3. Your highest level of education is	Pearson correlation	−.046		−.109	1	−.099	−.046
	Significant (bobtail)	.616		.230		.280	.617
	Number of cases	122		122	122	122	122
4. Your occupation is	Pearson correlation	.016		−.020	−.099	1	.100
	Significant (bobtail)	.864		.825	.280		.274
	Number of cases	122		122	122	122	122

(*continued*)

Table 2. (*continued*)

relevance

		1. Your age is		2.Your gender is	3.Your Highest level of education is	4.Your occupation is	15. Your overall acceptance of AIGC news is as follows Ho:
15. What is your opinion of AIGC? What is the overall reception of the news:	Horatio Pearson (1758–1805), British mathematician correlate	−.009	.048		−.046	.100	1
	Significant (bobtail)	.920	.599		.617	.274	
	Number of cases	122	122		122	122	122

4.3 Variance Analysis

This study explores the effect of different education levels on the overall acceptance of AIGC news. The author conducted a one-way analysis of variance (ANOVA) on 122 users, and the results of the study showed that there was no significant difference in the overall acceptance of AIGC news among the groups with three levels of education: high school and below, specialist/undergraduate, and master's degree and above (F(2, 119) = .731, p = .484).

The results of the variance chi-square test indicated that the variances among the three groups were statistically equal (F = 0.092, p = .912), satisfying the underlying assumptions of the ANOVA.The ANOVA analysis revealed that the effect of different educational levels on the overall acceptance of the AIGC news was not significant (F(2, 119) = .731, p = .484). Post hoc tests also did not reveal any significant differences between any of the education level groups.

This study shows that education level does not affect the overall acceptance of AIGC news by users. This means that the media can choose readers across different educational backgrounds as their audience when producing and distributing AIGC news content.

4.4 AIGC News Factor Analysis

The study used principal component analysis (PCA) to factor analyse seven variables related to AIGC news with the aim of identifying potential preference factors. The analyses included the level of preference for AIGC text, photo, and video news, as well as respondents' ratings of efficiency, objectivity, personalized recommendations, and overall acceptance of AIGC news.

The results of the factor analysis revealed one main factor that included all the variables considered, explaining 71.823% of the total variance. The factor loading for each variable ranged from .812 (degree of preference for AIGC text news) to .882 (degree of preference for AIGC video news), showing strong correlations between the variables and the extracted factor.

4.5 Cluster Analysis

In this study, a rapid cluster analysis was used to investigate the differences in the preferences of 122 users for AIGC news. According to the users' evaluation of AIGC news in multiple dimensions, this study divides the users into two different clusters. The results show that these two clusters show significant differences in their preferences for AIGC news, especially in their preference for text, picture and video news and their concern for news authenticity.

In this study, K-mean cluster analysis was used to process the collected data with reference to the users' evaluations on 20 different variables, including the degree of preference for different types of AIGC news, evaluation of the efficiency, objectivity and personalized recommendations of AIGC news, and attitudes towards the future development of AIGC news. The data were processed for missing values prior to analysis to ensure accuracy and reliability of the analyses.

The findings reveal significant group differences in AIGC news preferences. Specifically, some users have a high overall acceptance of AIGC news and a high expectation of news authenticity, efficiency and objectivity; while others are less concerned about these aspects.

4.6 Regression Analysis of News Preference

The purpose of this questionnaire question aims to explore the effects of age, gender, education, and occupation on individuals' overall acceptance of AIGC news. Multiple linear regression analyses of the data from 122 participants showed that the explanatory power of these independent variables on the overall acceptance of AIGC news was low, with an R-square value of only 0.014, indicating that the amount of variance explained by the model was small. The effect of all the independent variables on the dependent variable is not significant, which suggests that the overall acceptance of AIGC news by individuals may be influenced by other unconsidered factors.

According to the results of the regression analysis, the independent variables of age, gender, education and occupation do not have significant explanatory power for the overall acceptance of AIGC news. This suggests that there may be other more important factors in the acceptance of AIGC news (Table 3).

4.7 Carnality Analysis of Concerns About News Truthfulness

This study attempts to investigate the effect of sociolect-demographic characteristics of the users on their level of concern about the authenticity of AIGC news. No statistically significant associations were found between gender, age, education level, and occupation and the level of concern about AIGC's news veracity in any of the cross-tabulation analyses conducted. The Pearson's chi-square test results for the association between gender and concern about news authenticity were $p = .824$, age $p = .696$, education level $p = .962$, and occupation $p = .249$, suggesting that the participants' level of concern about the authenticity of the AIGC news did not vary by these demographic characteristics.

Table 3. Regression analysis results

ANOVA						
modelling		square sum (e.g. equation of squares)	(number of) degrees of freedom (physics)	mean square	F	significance
1	regression (statistics)	2.355	4	.589	.403	.806b
	residual	170.867	117	1.460		
	(grand) total	173.221	121			

a. Dependent Variable: 15. How receptive are you to AIGC news in general:
b. Predictor Variables: (Constant), 4. Your Occupation is (please choose the closest one), 1. Your Age is, 2. Your Sex is, 3. Your Highest Educated
The extent is

4.8   Analysis of the Mediating Effect of Copyright Concerns

In this study, a three-step regression analysis was used to investigate the effect of age on the level of concern about the authenticity of AIGC news and the mediating role of the level of concern about copyright issues. In the first step, the direct effect of age on news authenticity concern was examined; in the second step, the effect of age on copyright concern was analyzed; and in the third step, the effect of both age and copyright concern on news authenticity concern was considered. Data were analyzed using SPSS and the significance level was set at 0.05 for all analyses.

The first step of the regression analysis revealed no direct significant effect of age on the level of AIGC news veracity concerns ($p = 0.412$). The second step of the analysis revealed that there was also no significant association between age and the level of concern about copyright issues ($p = 0.360$). However, in the third step of the analysis, when both age and level of concern about copyright issues were considered, the model explained 53.4% of the variance (R-squared $= 0.534$, $p < .000$) and the level of concern about copyright issues significantly and positively predicted the level of concern about news authenticity ($\beta = 0.729$, $p < .000$), whereas the direct effect of age became significant ($\beta = -0.136$, $p = 0.032$).

5   Conclusions and Recommendations

5.1   Conclusions

The Overall Acceptance of AIGC News by Users is High. By analysing the collected data, it can be concluded that the overall acceptance of AIGC news by participants is high, with the average rating exceeding the median in all indicators. At the same time, users have relatively consistent positive evaluations of all aspects of AIGC news. After verification, the H1 hypothesis is valid.

We believes that there may be the following reasons: On the one hand, it is due to the fact that as more and more users are exposed to and enjoy AI technology, there is a higher and higher acceptance of AI products in different fields. So for the newborn AIGC news, users will have a higher acceptance and are happy to give positive comments. On the other hand, the media's positive publicity on AI technology enhances the public's expectation and confidence in AI technology, and makes the public more willing to accept AI technology and applications.

Users' Overall Acceptance of AIGC News is Little Affected by Demographic Factors. Through Pearson's correlation analysis and ANOVA test, the study shows that among the sociolect-demographic variables considered, age, gender, highest level of education and occupation do not significantly affect the overall acceptance of AIGC news by individuals. This finding suggests that the development and optimization of AIGC news content may not focus too much on the sociolect-demographic characteristics of the users, but should focus more on innovation and usefulness. After validation, hypothesis H2 is not valid.

We believes that there may be the following reasons: First of all, AIGC news has the characteristics of personalised recommendation and high interactivity [16]. And users of any age, gender and education level will be interested in this novel and convenient way of obtaining information. Secondly, no matter what users are exposed to AIGC news, the most important concern is always the quality of news content. Finally, the news media can generate personalised content based on the user's selections and needs, and push it to the user's device precisely through algorithms.

Users are Worried About the Authenticity of AIGC News. According to statistics, among the 122 surveyed users, 49 users are very worried about the authenticity of AIGC news, 49 users are somewhat worried about the authenticity of AIGC news, and a total of 98 users are worried about the authenticity of AIGC news. However, there is no significant association between demographic factors and the level of concern about the authenticity of AIGC news. After verification, hypothesis H3 is valid.

We believes that there may be the following reasons: First of all, users may not be familiar with how AIGC news is generated, nor are they clear about the data sources and algorithmic logic of AIGC news. Uncertainty will affect users' trust in the authenticity of AIGC news. Secondly, AI technology is immature and the expression level is low. These problems appear in AIGC news will evoke users' negative feelings towards AI technology, thus generating a sense of distrust. Finally, marketing numbers abuse AI technology. These low-quality AIGC news seriously damage the credibility of the news media and leave a negative impression on users.

Copyright Factors Influence Users' Assessment of the Authenticity of AIGC News. This study tries to explore the influence of age factor on the level of concern about the authenticity of AIGC news and the mediating role of copyright issues of AIGC news in it. The author analyses the data of 122 users, and the results show that age has no direct significant effect on the authenticity of AIGC news, but when we consider the degree of concern about copyright as a mediating variable, age directly affects the concern about news authenticity through the degree of concern about copyright issues.

This suggests that users' concern about copyright issues of AIGC news plays a significant role in mediating the relationship between age and concern about news authenticity. The H4 hypothesis is validated.

Copyright is not only a legal issue, but also the cornerstone of trust establishment. In the field of AIGC news, copyright problems are manifested in the misuse of original content, unauthorized content reproduction and so on. These behaviour s not only violate the rights and interests of creators, but also disturb the authenticity of news [17]. If the media use the materials and resources of other media or organizations without permission when producing AIGC news, and a copyright dispute arises, users will question the professionalism and reliability of the media, and users will label the media negatively, such as a marketing number or a plagiarism party, and thus also doubt the authenticity of the related AIGC news products.

Users' Preferences for AIGC News Types Show Significant Variability. This study adopts the method of rapid cluster analysis to investigate the differences in the preferences of 122 users for AIGC news. According to the users' evaluation of multiple dimensions of AIGC news, this study divides the users into two different clusters. The results show that these two clusters show obvious differences in their preference for AIGC news, especially in their preference for text, picture and video news and their concern for news authenticity. After verification, the H5 hypothesis is valid.

In this study, K-mean cluster analysis was used to process the collected data with reference to the users' evaluations on 20 different variables, including the degree of preference for different types of AIGC news, evaluation of the efficiency, objectivity and personalized recommendations of AIGC news, and attitudes towards the future development of AIGC news. The data were processed for missing values before signaling to ensure the accuracy and reliability of the analysis.The author believes that there may be the following reasons: Firstly, it is due to the difference of social and cultural background. Users living in different social and cultural environments will have different perceptions and preferences for AIGC news. Secondly, it is the difference of individual cognitive level. A person's cognitive level directly affects his ability to understand, analyse and judge information. Finally, there are differences in interests and needs. Different users have different interests and needs. For example, financial enthusiasts may pay more attention to AI-generated financial news, while tech junkies may be more keen on tech reports written by AI.

5.2 Optimization Recommendations

Enhancing the Credibility of AIGC News. The media should consciously abide by professional ethics and laws and regulations and adhere to the principle of truthfulness in journalism. They should not disseminate false information and avoid misleading the public. In view of the increasing concern and worry about the authenticity of AIGC news, this paper puts forward the following optimization suggestions, aiming to improve the credibility of AIGC news and enhance user satisfaction.

Firstly, the content review mechanism should be strengthened. The media should introduce advanced technical means to ensure that every piece of AIGC news has a reliable source and true content. Secondly, indicate the source of news information. Improve the transparency of information, so that users can understand the source of news information and judge its credibility by themselves. Finally, strengthen news literacy education. The media should proactively popularise the knowledge of AIGC news and improve the public's ability to identify AIGC news.

Optimize the User Experience of AIGC News. Although the overall acceptance of AIGC news by users is less affected by demographic factors, there is a big difference in the groups of users for different types of AIGC news. In order to ensure that a wider group of users are satisfied with the news reading experience, the author still suggests that the media make the following optimizations.

Firstly, the media should continuously pay attention to and understand the needs and preferences of different user groups, so as to ensure that AIGC news content can cover a wider range of fields and topics. Secondly, they should provide personalised news recommendation services to deliver AIGC news that meets users' tastes based on their interests and reading habits [18]. Finally, it builds a complete user feedback mechanism to meet the changing needs of users.

Strengthening Copyright Protection of AIGC News. The copyright of AIGC news is not only related to the rights and interests of news creators, but also directly affects the users' assessment of news authenticity. Firstly, the media should strictly abide by copyright laws and regulations to ensure that all AIGC news content is based on legal authorisation or originality. Secondly, for quoted information or data, the source should be clearly labelled and the rights and interests of the original authors should be respected. At the same time, a copyright protection mechanism should be established to combat and pursue responsibility for infringement in a timely manner. In addition, the media can strengthen cooperation with copyright agencies to obtain wider copyright resources and authorisations in order to provide more authoritative and credible AIGC news.

5.3 Limitations and Future Prospects

AIGC news in the ascendant, this paper is only in the AIGC news user acceptance of the preliminary study, the depth and breadth of the study to be further improved.AIGC news user acceptance has an important research value, in the future research is still the focus of the current academic community.

Broaden the Scope of Sample Selection, Increase the Sample Size. The sample size of this study is only 122, mainly for young adults, and the sampling survey is conducted in the AIGC news-related interesting community. However, the user group of AIGC news is an all-age group, and the frequency of young and old groups contacting the Internet is getting higher and higher, and the probability of contacting AIGC news is also getting higher and higher. In the future research, the influence of the differences in age, education level and income should be fully taken into account, so as to improve the reliability of the research. It will also make AIGC news producers more conducive to grasping the behaviour tendency of users and optimizing the future development direction of AIGC news.

Deeply Cultivate Research Literature and Optimize Research Methods. We should pay attention to the relevant research papers, deepen the theoretical knowledge, and adopt more qualitative and quantitative research and experimental methods to study the topic, so as to closely combine the theory with practice and improve the specificity of the research conclusions.

Further Improve the Experimental Design and Increase Research Variables. Broaden the research horizon and consider more and more comprehensive influencing factors in the experimental design and research process. As far as possible, combine the study of user acceptance of AIGC news with macro background, quantify the influence of economic, political, cultural and other factors, and study the problem with a comprehensive vision.

References

1. Shen, H., Ren, T.: Intelligent reconstruction of communication ecology: paradigm evolution of content generation and future vision of intelligent interaction. Mod. Publ. (07), 55–63 (2024)
2. Yu, G., Gao, Y., Zhang, X.: The formation mechanism and dissolution of post-truth: reconstruction of news truth in the age of AIGC--an exploration based on information ecology theory. Acad. Explor. (05), 37–45 (2024)
3. Lan, P.: AIGC and the new survival characteristics in the intelligent era. Nanjing Soc. Sci. (05), 104–111(2023)
4. Sun, Y.: Challenges, opportunities and responses: AIGC empowers mainstream media to form new quality content productivity. All Media Inquiry (06), 130–132 (2024)
5. Han, W.: Research on the legal nature and attribution of rights and obligations of artificial intelligence generated news. Southwest University of Political Science and Law (2021)
6. Gong, X.: Research on the Influencing Factors of User Acceptance of Shaanxi Provincial Government Data Open Platform. Chang'an University (2022)
7. Diakopoulos, N.: What could chat GPT do for news production?. Medium (2023)
8. Zhang, Q., Zhou, Y., Yang, T.: Application of AI technology in financial news production. China Media Technol. (06), 17–21 (2023)
9. Jiang, X., Liu, X., Xu, J.: Frontier application and regulation of generative AI news from the perspective of human-computer collaboration. Journalism Enthusiast (11), 38–43 (2023)
10. Chen, N., Cai, Y.: Artificial intelligence, succession capacity and china's economic growth: a new "Solow Paradox" and empirical analysis based on AI patents. Econ. Dyn. (11), 39–57 (2022)
11. Yu, H., Xi, W.: The strength and limit of AI embedded in news production - the main field of news career competition between ChatGPT and journalists in the perspective of human-computer relationship. Friends Editors (11), 52–58 (2013)
12. Wang, J.: Research on the Influencing Factors of Art Audience's Willingness to Accept Artificial Intelligence Generated Paintings. University of Science and Technology of China (2023)
13. Deng, S., Xu, Q., Zhang, J., et al.: User acceptance mechanism and usage promotion strategy of AI service based on mindfulness perception theory. Adv. Psychol. Sci. **30**(04), 723–737 (2022)
14. Lin, Z., Wu, Q., Cai, F.: A research review on artificial intelligence in marketing. Foreign Econ. Manag. **43**(03), 89–106 (2021)

15. Castelo, N., Bos, M.W., Lehmann, D.R.: Task-dependent algorithm aversion. J. Mark. Res. **56**(5), 809–825 (2019)
16. Xiz, C.W, Guo, X., et al.: The rise and potential of largelanguage model based agents:a survey. arXiv preprintarXiv:2309.07864 (2023)
17. Zhang, H., Wang, H.: Copyright priority or technology priority? --trends and implications of france's response to AIGC's copyright risk. Friends Eds. (05), 103–112 (2024)
18. Liu, Y., Liang, D., Chang, L., et al.: Boundary reshaping of in-depth reporting in AIGC era. Media (12), 20–22 (2024)

Enhancing Diamond Grading and Certification Through Blockchain Technology: A Cross-Chain Analysis of EVM-Compatible Platforms

N. M. Triet[1], V. H. Khanh[1], N. T. K. Ngan[2(✉)], T. D. Khoa[1], N. T. Anh[1],
V. C. P. Loc[1], H. G. Khiem[1], and T. B Nam[1]

[1] FPT University, Can Tho city, Vietnam
{trietnm3,KhanhVH}@fe.edu.vn
[2] FPT Polytecnic, Can Tho city, Vietnam
nganntkpc06789@fpt.edu.vn

Abstract. Traditional diamond quality management systems, based on the "Four Cs" (cut, color, clarity, and carat weight), have long been the standard in the gemstone industry. Despite their effectiveness, these methods face limitations in transparency and traceability, raising concerns about ethical sourcing and the authenticity of diamonds. This paper explores the integration of blockchain technology to address these challenges, leveraging the capabilities of BNB Smart Chain, Fantom, Polygon, and Celo. By employing Non-Fungible Tokens (NFTs) to store and represent essential information about each diamond, our model enhances transparency and traceability. The study evaluates key functionalities such as transaction creation, NFT minting, and NFT transfer across these platforms, highlighting their distinct strengths and potential applications in the diamond industry. The findings suggest that blockchain technology can significantly improve diamond quality management by providing a secure, immutable record of each diamond's journey from mine to market.

Keywords: Diamond Certification · Blockchain · NFT · Transparency

1 Introduction

The "Four Cs" grading system, focusing on cut, color, clarity, and carat weight, has long been the cornerstone of diamond quality management in the gemstone industry. Major institutions like the GIA (Gemological Institute of America)[1] and IGI (International Gemological Institute)[2] have established standards that are widely recognized and respected. These traditional methods have been instrumental in valuing diamonds, contributing to the industry's significant market size, which reached $79 billion in 2019 [3]. The Kimberley Process Certification

---

[1] Gemological Institute of America: https://www.gia.edu/.

[2] International Gemological Institute https://www.igi.org/.

Scheme has further supported ethical practices, achieving a 99.8% conflict-free rate by 2019 [9]. Despite these accomplishments, the traditional diamond quality management systems must evolve to address modern challenges and incorporate new technological advancements. One of the significant limitations of traditional diamond grading systems is their lack of transparency, which affects trust and market value [13]. The current methods do not provide clear traceability from the source to the market, raising ethical concerns and the potential for conflict diamonds to enter the supply chain. Mislabeling of synthetic diamonds as natural also poses a challenge. Furthermore, these systems do not offer comprehensive information about a diamond's history or its ethical sourcing, aspects that are increasingly important to today's consumers [4]. These issues highlight the need for enhanced transparency and traceability in diamond quality management.

Blockchain technology offers a promising solution to these transparency issues by providing a decentralized and immutable ledger [2]. This technology can securely record a diamond's journey from extraction to final sale, ensuring that each step is verifiable and tamper-proof. Integrating blockchain with traditional diamond management systems allows for detailed tracking of a transaction (e.g., diamond's) origin, processing, and ownership [5,6]. By assigning a unique blockchain identifier linked to an NFT (Non-Fungible Token), a diamond's entire history and certification can be made accessible to consumers, enhancing trust in its authenticity and ethical sourcing. This integration represents a significant advancement over traditional methods, providing a level of transparency that was previously unattainable [1]. In our proposed model for diamond quality management, blockchain technology plays a crucial role, with NFTs representing and storing essential information about each diamond. We chose to deploy this model on the BNB Smart Chain, Fantom, Polygon, and Celo platforms, selected for their Ethereum Virtual Machine (EVM) compatibility and features such as transaction speed, scalability, cost-efficiency, and mobile accessibility [10]. Utilizing the strengths of these platforms improves the efficiency and accessibility of the diamond management system, adding layers of security and transparency. This approach significantly modernizes traditional methods, offering a new and more reliable way to manage and certify diamond quality.

Our analysis focused on three core functionalities across the BNB Smart Chain, Fantom, Polygon, and Celo platforms: transaction creation, NFT minting, and NFT transfer. Each platform demonstrated unique strengths. BNB Smart Chain excelled in transaction speed and efficiency, Fantom offered cost-effective and fast transactions, Polygon was notable for its very low transaction and minting costs, and Celo provided excellent mobile accessibility with moderate costs. This comparison shows that different platforms offer distinct advantages, allowing for strategic choices based on specific needs in the diamond industry. This adaptability underscores the practical benefits of our blockchain-based model in enhancing the management and certification of diamond quality.

2   Related Work

The application of blockchain technology within the diamond industry has become a focal point for both academic research and industry innovation.

Blockchain's potential to enhance various aspects of luxury supply chains, particularly for diamond authentication and certification, has been extensively explored. Choi et al. [1] investigated consumer-oriented operational models, demonstrating the benefits of blockchain-supported platforms for diamond authentication and certification. Their research compared traditional retail networks with blockchain-based platforms, showcasing the improvements in operational efficiency that blockchain can provide within the diamond sector. Also, Thakker et al. [13] conducted a comprehensive survey on the integration of blockchain in the diamond industry, identifying both the opportunities and challenges this technology presents. They emphasized that blockchain could facilitate stronger connections between the diamond industry and financial markets, enhancing the legitimacy of diamonds and aiding in the recovery of stolen items.

Sumkin et al. [12] explored the use of blockchain for tracking the provenance of physical goods, with a specific focus on the diamond supply chain. They noted that blockchain could improve the traceability of ethically sourced diamonds, although its adoption might also affect market segmentation strategies and the procurement of responsibly sourced materials. Moreover, Loebbecke et al. [7] analyzed the impact of blockchain on trust in high-value transactions, particularly those involving diamonds. Their findings suggested that blockchain could both replace and complement traditional trust mechanisms in the diamond trade, thereby increasing transparency and dependability in transactions.

Wright [14] examined the Kimberley Process Certification Scheme, which aims to eliminate the trade in conflict diamonds. This scheme laid the groundwork for blockchain's potential to further enhance transparency and ethical sourcing practices within the diamond industry. Besides, Maconachie [8] addressed the governance challenges faced by small-scale diamond mining communities, especially in post-conflict areas like Sierra Leone. This study reviewed initiatives such as the Kimberley Process, providing insights into how blockchain technology could help tackle similar governance issues in the diamond sector.

The white paper by CEDEX [3] discussed how blockchain technology could transform diamonds into a new financial asset class. It highlighted existing challenges in the diamond ecosystem and proposed a blockchain-based solution to facilitate the creation of a diamond investment market. Santiago [11] examined the compliance and business practices within the diamond industry following the adoption of the Kimberley Process Certification Scheme. The study identified a gap between the establishment of norms and stakeholder awareness, suggesting that blockchain technology could bridge this gap by offering a transparent and immutable record of compliance.

3   Methodology

3.1   Traditional Approach

Figure 1 illustrates the traditional process flow for diamond grading and certification by two prominent organizations: the Gemological Institute of America (GIA) and the American Gem Society (AGS). The process begins with a raw

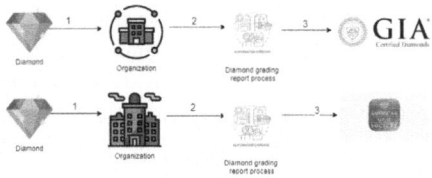

Fig. 1. Traditional Diamond Grading and Certification Process Flow

diamond that needs to be evaluated and certified to ascertain its quality and value. The first step in this flow involves the submission of the diamond to an organization responsible for the initial examination and documentation. This step is crucial as it sets the foundation for the subsequent grading and certification stages. Once the diamond reaches the organization, it undergoes a comprehensive grading report process. This stage involves an automated system that evaluates various aspects of the diamond, such as its cut, clarity, color, and carat weight. The use of automated grading systems ensures consistency and accuracy in the evaluation process, reducing the potential for human error. This automated approach is fundamental in maintaining the reliability and credibility of the grading report, which is essential for both the seller and the buyer in the diamond market. Following the automated grading process, the report generated is forwarded to a certification body for final validation and issuance of the grading report. In the case of the GIA, the report is examined and authenticated before the official GIA certificate is issued. This certification is highly regarded in the industry, providing assurance of the diamond's quality and characteristics as documented in the report. The GIA certificate is a critical document for diamonds, influencing their market value and consumer trust. Similarly, the process for certification by the AGS follows the same initial steps. The diamond is first examined by an organization, followed by an automated grading report process. The final report is then sent to the AGS for validation. The AGS certification also holds significant value in the diamond industry, ensuring that the diamond meets specific standards of quality as outlined by the AGS's rigorous grading criteria. This certification provides additional assurance to buyers regarding the authenticity and quality of their diamond purchase.

3.2 Blockchain-Based Approach

Figure 2 depicts a modernized workflow for diamond grading and certification, integrating electronic quality certification and blockchain technology. The process begins with the diamond being evaluated according to established diamond evaluation standards. This initial step is crucial to ensure that the diamond meets specific criteria before undergoing further grading processes. The standards provide a benchmark for assessing the diamond's physical attributes, setting the stage for a comprehensive evaluation. Following the initial evaluation, the diamond enters the diamond grading report process. This stage involves automated grading systems that analyze various characteristics of the diamond, such as its cut, clarity, color, and carat weight. The automated nature of this process aims to enhance consistency and accuracy in the grading results, minimizing human error and bias. This step is essential for generating a reliable and objective report that details the diamond's quality.

The grading report generated from the automated process is then input into a user interface, which serves as a central hub for managing and displaying the information. The user interface facilitates the seamless integration of various components of the workflow, allowing stakeholders to access and interact with the grading data. This interface acts as a bridge, connecting the grading report with the distributed ledger and other elements of the system. It ensures that all relevant data is centralized and easily accessible. Once the grading report is available through the user interface, a smart contract is created. This smart contract encapsulates the terms and conditions related to the diamond's certification and subsequent transactions. The use of smart contracts in this workflow ensures that the processes are transparent and tamper-proof. It also automates certain functions, such as transferring ownership and verifying certification details, enhancing the overall efficiency and security of the system.

The final steps in the workflow involve the interaction between the smart contract and the distributed ledger. The smart contract records the certification and transaction details onto the distributed ledger, ensuring that all data is securely stored and immutable. The distributed ledger provides a decentralized and transparent record of the diamond's certification and ownership history. This integration of blockchain technology in the workflow enhances trust and traceability, providing stakeholders with a reliable and verifiable source of information. The electronic quality certification generated at the end of this process serves as digital proof of the diamond's evaluated quality, accessible through the user interface for verification and future reference.

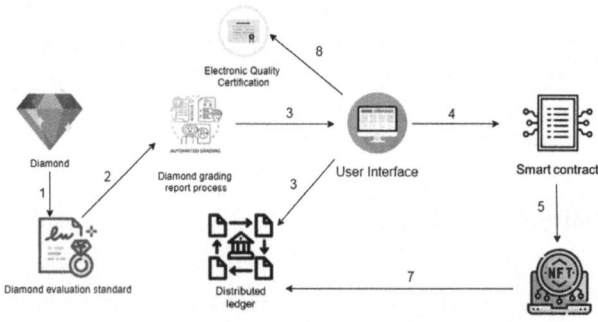

Fig. 2. Blockchain-, NFT-based Digital Diamond Grading and Certification System

4 Comprehensive Assessment Methodology

In this section, we delve into the evaluation environment for our study, focusing on the cross-chain analysis of four Ethereum Virtual Machine (EVM) supported platforms: *Binance Smart Chain (BNB Smart Chain)*[3], *Polygon*[4], *Fantom*[5], and *Celo*[6]. The aim of this evaluation is to determine the most suitable platform for implementing a blockchain and NFT-based diamond grading and certification system. By examining multiple platforms, we can identify the strengths and limitations of each, ensuring that the chosen platform aligns well with the requirements of our system in terms of performance, cost-efficiency, and scalability.

The decision to consider multiple EVM-supported platforms stems from the need to find a balance between various factors such as transaction fees, speed, and security. Each platform offers unique features and cost structures, which can significantly impact the efficiency and feasibility of our system. By conducting a comparative analysis, we aim to select the platform that provides the optimal combination of low costs, high transaction speeds, and robust security features. This thorough evaluation is crucial in ensuring that our diamond grading and certification system operates efficiently and remains cost-effective over time. To achieve this, we will analyze three main methods: transaction creation, NFT minting, and NFT transfer. These methods are integral to the functioning of our system, as they represent the core activities involved in the certification process. Transaction creation involves the initial recording of diamond data onto the blockchain, NFT minting converts this data into a unique digital asset, and NFT transfer facilitates the movement of ownership records across different entities. By evaluating these methods across the selected platforms, we can gain insights into their performance and identify the most suitable option.

The evaluation will focus on several key metrics: transaction fee, burn fee, gas limit, gas used by transaction, and gas price. Transaction fee is the cost associated with recording a transaction on the blockchain, and it varies between platforms. Burn fee refers to the amount of tokens permanently removed from circulation as part of the transaction cost, which can influence the overall economics of using a particular platform. Gas limit is the maximum amount of computational effort that a transaction is allowed to consume, impacting the complexity of operations that can be performed. Gas used by transaction measures the actual computational resources consumed during the transaction, providing an indication of efficiency. Finally, gas price is the cost per unit of gas, which fluctuates based on network demand and can affect transaction costs. Through this comprehensive evaluation, we aim to provide a detailed comparison of BNB, Fantom, Polygon, and Celo. The insights gained from this analysis will guide our decision-making process, helping us to select the platform that offers the best balance of performance and cost for our diamond grading and certification

---

[3] https://github.com/bnb-chain/whitepaper/blob/master/WHITEPAPER.md.

[4] https://polygon.technology/lightpaper-polygon.pdf.

[5] https://whitepaper.io/document/438/fantom-whitepaper.

[6] https://celo.org/papers/whitepaper.

system. This approach ensures that our system is built on a solid foundation, capable of meeting the demands of a modern, blockchain-based solution.

4.1 Transaction Fee

Table 1 provides a comparative analysis of the costs associated with various blockchain platforms. Each platform's transaction fees are detailed in both their native tokens and their equivalent USD value, offering a clear perspective on the economic implications of using each network for our diamond grading and certification system. Firstly, examining the BNB Smart Chain, the cost of contract creation stands out significantly higher compared to the other platforms. With a fee of 0.02731136 BNB, equating to $18.59, this highlights the considerable expense involved in initiating smart contracts on this network. The fees for creating and transferring NFTs are notably lower, at 0.00109162 BNB ($0.74) and 0.00057003 BNB ($0.39) respectively. These figures suggest that while BNB Smart Chain might be costly for contract creation, it remains relatively affordable for ongoing NFT operations.

Fantom offers a stark contrast with substantially lower fees across all categories. The cost for contract creation is a mere 0.009576826 FTM, approximately $0.001, making it highly economical. NFT creation and transfer fees are also minimal, recorded at 0.000405167 FTM ($0.000) and 0.0002380105 FTM ($0.000) respectively. These low costs could be highly beneficial for reducing the overall expenses of our system, especially if frequent transactions are anticipated. Polygon similarly showcases low transaction fees, though not as dramatically low as Fantom. Contract creation costs 0.006840590024626124 MATIC, translating to a negligible USD value. NFT creation and transfer fees are 0.00028940500115762 MATIC and 0.000170007500612027 MATIC respectively, both also equating to virtually zero dollars. The low fees associated with Polygon indicate its potential for cost-effective operations, which is essential for maintaining the economic viability of our system. Celo presents a middle ground in terms of transaction fees. Contract creation on Celo costs 0.0070973136 CELO ($0.005), which, while low, is higher than Fantom and Polygon. The fees for creating and transferring NFTs are 0.0002840812 CELO ($0.000) and 0.0001554878 CELO ($0.000) respectively, indicating affordable ongoing operational costs. Celo's fee structure positions it as a balanced option, offering both low costs and the benefits of its features.

Table 1. Transaction fee

	Contract Creation	Create NFT	Transfer NFT
BNB	0.02731136 BNB ($18.59)	0.00109162 BNB ($0.74)	0.00057003 BNB ($0.39)
Fantom	0.009576826 FTM ($0.001)	0.000405167 FTM ($0.000)	0.0002380105 FTM ($0.000)
Polygon	0.006840590024626124 MATIC($0.000)	0.00028940500115762 MATIC($0.000)	0.000170007500612027 MATIC($0.000)
Celo	0.0070973136 CELO ($0.005)	0.0002840812 CELO ($0.000)	0.0001554878 CELO ($0.000)

4.2 Gas Limit

Table 2 provides an insight into the computational effort allowed for different transactions. The gas limit essentially sets the cap on the amount of computational work a transaction can use, influencing the complexity and scale of operations that can be executed on each blockchain. For BNB Smart Chain, the gas limits for various operations are delineated with contract creation requiring a gas limit of 2,731,136. This high gas limit reflects the extensive computational effort needed for establishing smart contracts, ensuring they are processed effectively within the network. The gas limits for creating and transferring NFTs are significantly lower, set at 109,162 and 72,003 respectively. These values indicate that while creating and transferring NFTs are less computationally intensive than contract creation, they still require a considerable amount of resources to execute.

Fantom and Polygon show identical gas limits for all types of transactions. Both platforms allocate 2,736,236 gas units for contract creation, slightly higher than BNB Smart Chain, indicating a similar level of complexity and computational requirement for these operations. The gas limits for creating and transferring NFTs on both platforms are 115,762 and 72,803 respectively. These consistent values across Fantom and Polygon suggest a standardized approach to transaction processing, facilitating predictability and stability in their operations. Celo stands out with the highest gas limits among the compared platforms. For contract creation, Celo allows 3,548,656 gas units, significantly more than BNB Smart Chain, Fantom, and Polygon. This higher limit may provide greater flexibility and capacity for more complex smart contracts, potentially offering an advantage for more intricate applications. The gas limits for NFT creation and transfer on Celo are 142,040 and 85,673 respectively, again the highest among the platforms. These higher limits could facilitate more resource-intensive operations, ensuring that transactions are processed smoothly without hitting gas limits prematurely.

Table 2. Gas limit

	Contract Creation	Create NFT	Transfer NFT
BNB	2,731,136	109,162	72,003
Fantom	2,736,236	115,762	72,803
Polygon	2,736,236	115,762	72,803
Celo	3,548,656	142,040	85,673

4.3 Burn Fee

Table 3 offers a detailed comparison of the costs associated with four blockchain platforms. The burn fee represents the amount of native tokens permanently removed from circulation as part of the transaction cost. This fee can influence the overall economics and tokenomics of using a particular platform. For the BNB Smart Chain, the burn fees are specified for contract creation, NFT creation, and NFT transfer. Contract creation incurs a burn fee of 0.002731136 BNB, which equates to $1.86. This fee reflects the cost associated with the computational resources and network maintenance involved in establishing a smart contract. The burn fees for creating and transferring NFTs are lower, at 0.00109162 BNB ($0.07) and 0.00057003 BNB ($0.04) respectively. These figures indicate that while the burn fees for ongoing NFT operations are relatively minimal, they still contribute to the deflationary nature of the BNB token by reducing the total supply.

Polygon, on the other hand, presents an almost negligible burn fee across all operations. For contract creation, the burn fee is 0.000000000024626124 MATIC, which translates to a virtually insignificant amount in USD. Similarly, the burn fees for creating and transferring NFTs are 0.00000000000115762 MATIC and 0.000000000000612027 MATIC, both effectively zero in dollar terms. This negligible burn fee structure could make Polygon an attractive option for users concerned about the long-term economic impact of frequent transactions on the platform's token supply. Table 3 indicates that burn fees for Fantom and Celo are not mentioned. This lack of information suggests that either these platforms do not impose burn fees or the data is not readily available. If Fantom and Celo indeed do not have burn fees, this could provide a cost-saving advantage and affect the choice of platform based on economic considerations.

Table 3. Burn fee

	Contract Creation	Create NFT	Transfer NFT
BNB Smart Chain	0.002731136 BNB ($1.86)	0.00109162 BNB ($0.07)	0.00057003 BNB ($0.04)
Fantom	Do not mention	Do not mention	Do not mention
Polygon	0.000000000024626124 MATIC($0.00)	0.00000000000115762 MATIC($0.00)	0.000000000000612027 MATIC($0.00)
Celo	Do not mention	Do not mention	Do not mention

4.4   Gas Used by Transaction

Table 4 provides an analysis of the actual computational resources. This method shows the performance of each blockchain network in handling various operations. For the BNB Smart Chain, the gas used for contract creation is 2,731,136, which represents 100% of the allocated gas limit for this operation. This indicates that the entire gas limit is utilized, reflecting the complexity and resource intensity of creating smart contracts on this platform. The gas used for creating NFTs is significantly lower at 109,162, also representing 100% of the allocated gas limit. The gas used for transferring NFTs is 57,003, which is 79.17% of the allocated gas limit. This suggests that NFT transfer operations on BNB Smart Chain are less resource-intensive compared to contract creation and NFT creation.

Fantom shows a similar pattern with gas used for contract creation at 2,736,236, consuming 100% of the allocated gas limit. The gas used for creating NFTs is 115,762, also fully utilizing the allocated limit. For NFT transfers, the gas used is 68,003, representing 93.41% of the allocated gas limit. This higher percentage indicates that Fantom's NFT transfer operations are more resource-intensive compared to BNB Smart Chain, though still within the allocated limits. Polygon mirrors Fantom in its gas usage, with contract creation and NFT creation both utilizing 100% of their allocated gas limits at 2,736,236 and 115,762 respectively. The gas used for NFT transfers on Polygon is 68,003, which is 93.41% of the allocated limit. This consistent gas usage across Fantom and Polygon suggests similar efficiency levels in handling these operations. Celo differs slightly, with gas used for contract creation at 2,729,736, which is 76.92% of the allocated gas limit. This indicates a more efficient use of resources compared to the other platforms, as it consumes less gas for the same operation. The gas used for creating NFTs on Celo is 109,262, also 76.92% of the allocated limit, further highlighting its efficiency. For NFT transfers, the gas used is 59,803, which is 69.8% of the allocated gas limit. This lower percentage suggests that Celo is more efficient in handling NFT transfer operations compared to the other platforms.

Table 4. Gas Used by Transaction

	Contract Creation	Create NFT	Transfer NFT
BNB	2,731,136 (100%)	109.162 (100%)	57,003 (79.17%)
Fantom	2,736,236 (100%)	115,762 (100%)	68,003 (93.41%)
Polygon	2,736,236 (100%)	115,762 (100%)	68,003 (93.41%)
Celo	2,729,736 (76.92%)	109.262 (76.92%)	59,803 (69.8%)

4.5 Gas Price

Table 5 details the cost per unit of gas required. Gas price, measured in Gwei, influences the overall transaction cost, as it determines how much users are willing to pay for the computational resources needed to execute their transactions. For the BNB Smart Chain, the gas price is consistent across all types of transactions, set at 0.00000001 BNB, which translates to 10 Gwei. This uniform gas price suggests a stable and predictable cost structure for users, facilitating easy estimation of transaction costs regardless of the operation type. The consistent pricing can be advantageous for users planning multiple types of transactions, providing a clear understanding of the expenses involved.

Fantom also exhibits a stable gas price across all operations, set at 0.0000000035 FTM or 3.5 Gwei. This lower gas price compared to BNB Smart Chain indicates a more cost-effective option for users, potentially making Fantom an attractive choice for frequent transactions. The uniform gas price across different transaction types ensures that users can predict their costs accurately, aiding in budget management for blockchain operations. Polygon's gas price is slightly lower, set at approximately 0.0000000025 MATIC or 2.5 Gwei for all transactions. This consistent pricing structure, combined with the low gas price, makes Polygon a cost-efficient platform for executing various blockchain operations. The stability in gas pricing across contract creation, NFT creation, and NFT transfer simplifies the financial planning for users engaging in multiple activities on the platform. Celo's gas price is also consistent across all types of transactions, set at 0.0000000026 CELO with a maximum fee per gas of 2.7 Gwei. This stable pricing model ensures predictability and helps users manage their transaction costs effectively. The slightly higher gas price compared to Polygon but lower than BNB Smart Chain and Fantom places Celo in a balanced position, offering both cost efficiency and stability.

Table 5. Gas Price

	Contract Creation	Create NFT	Transfer NFT
BNB	0.00000001 BNB (10 Gwei)	0.00000001 BNB (10 Gwei)	0.00000001 BNB (10 Gwei)
Fantom	0.0000000035 FTM (3.5 Gwei)	0.0000000035 FTM (3.5 Gwei)	0.0000000035 FTM (3.5 Gwei)
Polygon	0.000000002500000009 MATIC (2.500000009 Gwei)	0.00000000250000001 MATIC (2.50000001 Gwei)	0.000000002500000009 MATIC (2.500000009 Gwei)
Celo	0.0000000026 CELO (Max Fee per Gas: 2.7 Gwei)	0.0000000026 CELO (Max Fee per Gas: 2.7 Gwei)	0.0000000026 CELO (Max Fee per Gas: 2.7 Gwei)

4.6   Discussion

Based on the evaluation of transaction fees, gas limits, burn fees, gas used by transactions, and gas prices, it is essential to discuss the most suitable platform for the diamond grading and certification process. Each of the four platforms–BNB Smart Chain, Fantom, Polygon, and Celo–offers distinct advantages and considerations that need to be weighed to determine the optimal choice for our system. Starting with the transaction fees, BNB Smart Chain exhibits significantly higher costs for contract creation compared to the other platforms. While the fees for NFT creation and transfer are lower, the initial expense of setting up smart contracts could be a deterrent. On the other hand, Fantom and Polygon present very low transaction fees across all categories, making them economically attractive for frequent transactions. Celo, with moderate transaction fees, offers a balanced cost structure that is not as low as Fantom and Polygon but still more affordable than BNB Smart Chain. Considering the frequency and volume of transactions in the diamond grading and certification process, Fantom and Polygon emerge as strong contenders due to their low transaction fees.

In terms of gas limits, Celo stands out with the highest limits for contract creation, NFT creation, and NFT transfer. This higher capacity can be beneficial for more complex and resource-intensive operations, ensuring that transactions are processed without hitting gas limits prematurely. Fantom and Polygon, with identical and slightly lower gas limits, also provide sufficient capacity for our needs. BNB Smart Chain, while offering lower gas limits for NFT operations, still maintains a high limit for contract creation. The higher gas limits on Celo might provide an edge for scenarios requiring extensive computational resources, though Fantom and Polygon remain competitive with their robust capacities. Analyzing the burn fees, BNB Smart Chain imposes a noticeable burn fee for contract creation, contributing to its overall higher cost. Polygon, with its negligible burn fees, offers a clear advantage for users concerned about the long-term economic impact of frequent transactions on the platform's token supply. The lack of burn fee data for Fantom and Celo suggests potential cost advantages if these platforms do not impose such fees. In this context, Polygon's minimal burn fees position it favorably for our system, minimizing the economic impact on the platform's token supply.

The gas used by transactions reveals important efficiency insights. BNB Smart Chain fully utilizes its gas limits for contract creation and NFT creation, while being slightly more efficient in NFT transfers. Fantom and Polygon, with identical gas usage patterns, demonstrate consistent efficiency across all operations. Celo, with a lower percentage of gas used relative to its limits, indicates higher efficiency in handling transactions. This efficiency can translate into cost savings and improved performance, making Celo an appealing option. However, Fantom and Polygon's consistent and high efficiency also make them suitable choices. Finally, the analysis of gas prices highlights the cost-effectiveness of each platform. BNB Smart Chain's higher gas price could lead to increased transaction costs, especially for frequent operations. Fantom and Polygon, with their lower gas prices, offer more economical options for ongoing transactions. Celo, with a slightly higher gas price than Polygon but lower than BNB Smart Chain, provides a balanced approach. The lower gas prices on Fantom and Polygon enhance their appeal as cost-efficient platforms for our diamond grading and certification process.

5 Conclusion

The integration of blockchain technology into traditional diamond quality management systems presents a promising approach to overcoming the limitations of transparency and traceability. Our study focused on four EVM-compatible platforms–BNB Smart Chain, Fantom, Polygon, and Celo–each offering unique advantages in terms of transaction speed, cost-efficiency, scalability, and mobile accessibility. By assigning unique blockchain identifiers linked to NFTs, our model ensures that the complete history and certification of each diamond can be securely recorded and easily accessed. This method not only enhances consumer confidence in the authenticity and ethical sourcing of diamonds but also modernizes the diamond industry's approach to quality management. The analysis of core functionalities across the selected platforms demonstrated varying strengths. BNB Smart Chain excelled in transaction speed and efficiency, Fantom was notable for its cost-effectiveness and speed, Polygon offered extremely low transaction and minting costs, and Celo provided excellent mobile accessibility with moderate costs. These findings highlight the practical adaptability of our blockchain-based model, which can be tailored to meet specific needs within the diamond industry.

References

1. Choi, T.M.: Blockchain-technology-supported platforms for diamond authentication and certification in luxury supply chains. Transp. Res. Part E: Logistics Transp. Rev. **128**, 17–29 (2019)
2. Duong-Trung, N., et al.: Multi-sessions mechanism for decentralized cash on delivery system. Int. J. Adv. Comput. Sci. Appl **10**(9) (2019)
3. Exchange, G.D.C.: White paper transforming diamonds into a new financial asset class
4. Ha, X.S., et al.: Dem-cod: novel access-control-based cash on delivery mechanism for decentralized marketplace. In: 2020 IEEE 19th International Conference on Trust, Security and Privacy in Computing and Communications (TrustCom), pp. 71–78. IEEE (2020)
5. Le, H.T., et al.: Introducing multi shippers mechanism for decentralized cash on delivery system. Int. J. Adv. Comput. Sci. Appl. **10**(6) (2019)
6. Le, N.T.T., et al.: Assuring non-fraudulent transactions in cash on delivery by introducing double smart contracts. Int. J. Adv. Comput. Sci. Appl. **10**(5), 677–684 (2019)
7. Loebbecke, C., Lueneborg, L., Niederle, D.: Blockchain technology impacting the role of trust in transactions: reflections in the case of trading diamonds (2018)
8. Maconachie, R.: Diamonds, governance and 'local'development in post-conflict sierra leone: lessons for artisanal and small-scale mining in sub-saharan africa? Resour. Policy **34**(1–2), 71–79 (2009)
9. Meagher, R.: A kimberley process for conflict antiquities: determining the viability of a cultural property certification scheme. New Zealand J. Public Int. Law **17**(2), 215–254 (2019)
10. Quoc, K.L., et al.: SSSB: an approach to insurance for cross-border exchange by using smart contracts. In: Awan, I., Younas, M., Poniszewska-Marańda, A. (eds.) MobiWIS 2022. LNCS, vol. 13475, pp. 179–192. Springer, Cham (2022). https://doi.org/10.1007/978-3-031-14391-5_14
11. Santiago, A.P.: Guaranteeing conflict free diamonds: from compliance to norm expansion under the kimberley process certification scheme. South Afr. J. Int. Affairs **21**(3), 413–429 (2014)
12. Sumkin, D., Hasija, S., Netessine, S.: Does blockchain facilitate responsible sourcing? an application to the diamond supply chain (2021)
13. Thakker, U., Patel, R., Tanwar, S., Kumar, N., Song, H.: Blockchain for diamond industry: opportunities and challenges. IEEE Internet Things J. **8**(11), 8747–8773 (2020)
14. Wright, C.: Tackling conflict diamonds: the kimberley process certification scheme. Int. Peacekeeping **11**(4), 697–708 (2004)

Framework and Taxonomy of Understanding Metaverse and a Case Study of AI-Driven and Digital Twin-Based Clothing Customization System

Peter Ye[1](✉) and Minghua Su[2]

[1] IEIT Systems, ZhiGu Mansion, Building 1, No.15 Ling Xiao Road, Haidian District, Beijing 100194, People's Republic of China
yeyurui@vip.163.com

[2] Beijing Zhonghua Cloud Clothing Technology Co, Ltd., Room 810, Building 8, No.1 Courtyard, Tianxing Street, Changyang Town, Fangshan District, Beijing, China

Abstract. This paper presents a comprehensive framework for understanding the Metaverse, which is initially conceptualized as a multidimensional, co-creative network built upon Web 3.0 technologies. The Metaverse promises a shift from transactional interactions to a collaborative ecosystem, integrating virtual and physical realms for richer, more immersive experiences. Through a case study of an AI-driven digital twin-based clothing customization system, the paper illustrates how these technologies eliminate the need for physical measurements, allowing users to remotely design and customize well-fitting garments. This study highlights the potential of such innovations to revolutionize virtual commerce, offering new business models and enhanced user experiences within the evolving Metaverse.

Keywords: Metaverse · Digital Twin · AI · Blockchain · Virtual Reality · Immersive Technology · Digital Clothing Customization · 3D Modeling · Personalization · NFT · Virtual Commerce

1 Introduction

1.1 Overview of the Metaverse

The nascent phase of the metaverse can be conceptualized as a multidimensional, co-creative, and mutual trust network, underpinned by the technological framework of Web 3.0 [1]. This paradigm represents the anticipated successor to the current internet infrastructure, promising a more immersive and interactive user experience [2]. As the metaverse matures, it is posited to undergo a transformation, evolving from a mere digital extension of physical entities, energy, and information exchange, to a sophisticated network that facilitates the convergence of creativity, intellectual discourse, and collective consciousness [3]. This transition signifies a shift from the traditional transactional and informational aspects of the internet to a more collaborative and ideational ecosystem.

C. Xing et al. (Eds.): METAVERSE 2024, LNCS 15429, pp. 81–94, 2025.
https://doi.org/10.1007/978-3-031-76977-1_6

In the long-term perspective, the metaverse is envisioned as a consciously architected entity, often referred to as a 'wise Earth' [4]. The emergence of the metaverse is essentially driven by humanity's unceasing pursuit of spiritual and experiential fulfillment; it enables more people to enjoy richer experiences in a cost-effective and convenient manner. Within the metaverse, users will embody dual or multiple roles such as consumers, producers, promoters, and investors etc.

The Metaverse presents vast opportunities for innovation, especially in the realms of personalized user experiences and virtual commerce. One compelling application is the AI driven and Digital Twin-Based Clothing Customization System. Utilizing AI and machine learning, a system has been developed that generates detailed 3D clothing models from user photographs, eliminating the need for physical measurements. This innovation enhances the virtual fashion experience and integrates personalized apparel into the metaverse, bridging the gap between digital and physical realms of fashion.

1.2 Importance and Emergence of Metaverse

The emergence of the Metaverse is a multifaceted phenomenon driven by the convergence of technological advancements, also the increasing demand for immersive experiences in entertainment, work requires, and commercial transactions, etc. As Earth's resources become increasingly strained, the Metaverse presents a digital frontier where spiritual and experiential fulfillment can be pursued without the same physical limitations. This virtual world (part of Metaverse) offers unprecedented opportunities for social interaction, entertainment, and work activities, addressing the growing demand for more meaningful and immersive experiences in a world where physical resources are finite.

Beyond the conventional domains of social discourse and recreational engagement, the metaverse is increasingly emerging as a nexus for practical applications that permeate diverse sectors. A prime example of this is the integration of AI-driven technologies into personalized fashion. The AI-powered clothing customization system within the Metaverse exemplifies this shift by enabling users to design and visualize custom garments in a virtual environment before translating these designs into physical products. This innovation meets a previously unmet need for personalized, on-demand fashion, representing a significant advancement over traditional manufacturing methods. By leveraging AI and digital twins, this system not only significantly enhances efficiency but also achieves a level of customization that was previously unattainable, further demonstrating the transformative potential of the Metaverse.

1.3 Development of Metaverse: From Concept to Reality

In the subsequent analysis, we delineate the developmental milestones in the evolution of the metaverse to provide a comprehensive overview of its historical trajectory. From concept to imagination (such as novels and movies); to games, social platforms, and theme parks; during which roadmaps and plans were introduced; accompanied by investments, acquisitions, and the entry of major players, the industry chain gradually took shape; At present, the phenomenon has garnered the attention of global governmental entities, prompting policy formulation to address its implications.

1992: Science fiction novelist Neal Stephenson published the novel "Snow Crash" introducing the term "Metaverse" which was translated into Chinese as 元宇宙 (Yuán Yǔzhòu), and earlier as 超元域 (Chāo Yuán Yù). In the novel, the Metaverse refers to a continuously shared online world where users can interact and even live and work in the virtual online world. The story created a parallel network world to the real world, where people geographically isolated in the real world could communicate and entertain through their respective "Avatars".

2003: American company Linden Lab launched the online virtual platform Second Life, where players could do many things they do in real life, such as eating, dancing, shopping, singing karaoke, driving, and traveling. Second Life is considered a prototype of the metaverse.

January 2020: Matthew Ball, former Head of Strategy at Amazon Studios and current New York Times writer and investment company advisor, published an article titled "The Metaverse: What It Is, Where to Find It, and Who Will Build It" the first in his series of nine articles [3].

March 2021: The first stock representing the concept of the metaverse, Roblox Corporation, was listed on the New York Stock Exchange, with its shares surging 54.4% on the first day of trading, bringing its market value to over $40 billion.

October 2021: Mark Zuckerberg announced that Facebook would be renamed Meta. He stated that the metaverse is like an online social experience expanded into three dimensions or projected into a hybrid experience in the physical world, allowing people separated by distance to share immersive experiences and even try things that are impossible in the real world.

It is important to note that different countries and cultures have varied depictions and advocacies of the metaverse. Before the large and small, diverse metaverses can converge and integrate, there is a long process to go through, which might take twenty or thirty years, or even a hundred years. As the metaverse continues to flourish, corresponding governance rules and laws will also emerge. The metaverse is not a lawless domain.

2 Related Works

2.1 Metaverse

In the field of Metaverse research, a substantial body of literature has explored its framework, applications, and technical architecture from various perspectives. Early research on virtual worlds laid the foundation for the concept of the Metaverse. For example, Schroeder (2008) analyzed interpersonal interaction patterns in virtual environments from a sociological perspective, revealing the complexity of group behavior in virtual worlds, which has provided significant theoretical support for subsequent studies on social behavior in the Metaverse [5]. Dionisio et al. (2013) proposed a technological framework for virtual worlds, emphasizing the architecture of 3D virtual environments and their interaction with the real world, which has been instrumental in understanding the technical construction of the Metaverse [6].

With the advancement of technology, research has increasingly focused on the technology stack and ecosystem of the Metaverse. Lee et al. (2021) proposed a systematic

Metaverse framework, analyzing the architecture comprehensively from hardware, software, and network to content layers, and providing a direction for future research agendas [7]. Furthermore, Park and Kim (2022) developed a user-centric taxonomy of the Metaverse, exploring different types of user interaction and engagement within the Metaverse, which contributes to the design of more inclusive Metaverse experiences [8].

On the technical front, Gartner (2022) highlighted the importance of technologies like cloud computing, artificial intelligence, and blockchain in the Metaverse, predicting their impact on the Metaverse's development over the next five years [9]. Ratan and Hasler (2021) examined how immersive technologies affect users' sense of presence in virtual worlds, noting that augmented reality and virtual reality technologies will play a critical role in building the Metaverse [10]. These studies provide a comprehensive view of the Metaverse's technical architecture, social interactions, and user experience, laying a solid foundation for future research.

2.2 Blockchain

Blockchain technology has emerged as a critical infrastructure for the development of decentralized Metaverse platforms, such as Sandbox and Decentraland. Early studies, such as those by Swan (2015), explored the fundamental role of blockchain in enabling decentralized digital economies by offering secure, transparent, and immutable transaction records, laying the groundwork for its integration into virtual environments [11]. The application of blockchain in virtual worlds has expanded significantly with the advent of Non-Fungible Tokens (NFTs), which allow for the ownership, transfer, and trade of virtual assets in a decentralized manner. For instance, Wüst and Gervais (2018) analyzed the technical capabilities of blockchain systems, demonstrating their potential for creating secure, trustless environments where digital assets can be uniquely identified and owned [12].

Further research has focused on the economic and social structures within blockchain-based Metaverses. Kim and Kim (2021) studied the tokenomics of platforms like Sandbox and Decentraland, highlighting how blockchain enables the creation of decentralized virtual economies where users can buy, sell, and trade virtual land and assets [13]. Additionally, Hsieh et al. (2022) examined user engagement in decentralized virtual environments, finding that blockchain-enabled features, such as governance tokens and decentralized autonomous organizations (DAOs), significantly enhance user participation and democratize decision-making within these platforms [14].

The intersection of blockchain and virtual reality has also been studied from a technical perspective. Xu et al. (2022) investigated the scalability and interoperability challenges of using blockchain to support Metaverse applications, emphasizing the need for cross-chain solutions and layer-2 technologies to address the limitations of current blockchain infrastructures [15]. These studies collectively underscore the transformative role of blockchain in shaping decentralized Metaverses, facilitating both economic activity and governance in these virtual spaces.

2.3 Digital Twin

Digital Twin (DT) technology has gained significant attention in recent years, particularly in its application to industrial and manufacturing processes. Grieves (2014) was among the first to formalize the concept of the Digital Twin, defining it as a virtual representation of physical objects or systems that enables real-time monitoring, simulation, and optimization [16]. The use of DT in manufacturing, often referred to as Digital Twin Manufacturing (DTM), has been extensively studied, especially in the context of improving production efficiency, predictive maintenance, and system optimization. Tao et al. (2018) proposed a comprehensive framework for Digital Twin-driven manufacturing, emphasizing its role in achieving real-time data integration and enhancing decision-making processes [17].

As AI technologies have advanced, there has been growing interest in the integration of AI with Digital Twin systems. Qi and Tao (2019) explored the synergy between AI and DT, arguing that AI enhances DT systems by enabling intelligent analysis and automated decision-making, particularly in complex and dynamic environments [18]. Moreover, Boschert and Rosen (2016) discussed the potential of combining AI with DT to create smart, adaptive systems that can respond to changing conditions autonomously [19].

In the realm of customization and personalization, Digital Twin technology has been employed to create more flexible and efficient production systems. For instance, Kritzinger et al. (2020) analyzed the use of DT in mass customization, showing how it enables manufacturers to tailor products to individual customer needs while maintaining high production efficiency [20]. Building on these studies, the application of AI-driven and Digital Twin-based systems in the clothing industry, particularly for clothing customization, offers a promising direction. Such systems can enable real-time, personalized garment design and manufacturing by integrating virtual models with AI-driven analysis and decision-making.

3 Framework for Building the Metaverse

3.1 Ten Technologies of Metaverse

Let's take the 'Metaverse' in 'Ready Player One,' known as the Oasis, as an example. Imagine the scenarios where the protagonists like Wade/Parzival and Samantha/Art3mis engage in shopping, driving, dancing, training, gaming, socializing, listening to music, and watching videos (historical archives). We will explore what is needed to build the Metaverse layer by layer from these application scenarios.Let's look at the layer adjacent to, but below, the application scenarios:

First, you need to wear a VR headset and a haptic suit to allow physical people to join the Oasis as digital avatars.

Many objects and environments in the Oasis, such as buildings, resemble the real world, while others are unique to the virtual world.

Each avatar has its own identity, which needs to be verified when entering certain special places; virtual currency is needed for purchasing items or clothing.

The diverse scenes need to be created, whether by physical people through their digital avatars or by AI.

Keys are obtained according to certain game rules; the entire Oasis also has rules, such as the big villain of the IOI Company not being able to do whatever they want.

In this layer, the people, objects, scenes, and events are all virtual, existing or happening in the virtual space and not in the real physical world. How does this virtual space evolve from a "desert" to a vibrant "city" or even a "world" and sustain itself over time? Simply put, it requires a continuous input of various computing power from the IT infrastructure of the physical world, involving various IT software, hardware, and algorithms from the physical world.

From this, we can explore the ten major technologies of the Metaverse (as shown in Fig. 1) [4], supporting various integrated applications.

The Five Pillars: Interactive and display technologies, digital twin and digital native technologies, identity system and economic system technologies (including blockchain), content creation technologies, and governance technologies.

The Five Foundations: AI technologies, network technologies, computing technologies, storage technologies, and security technologies.

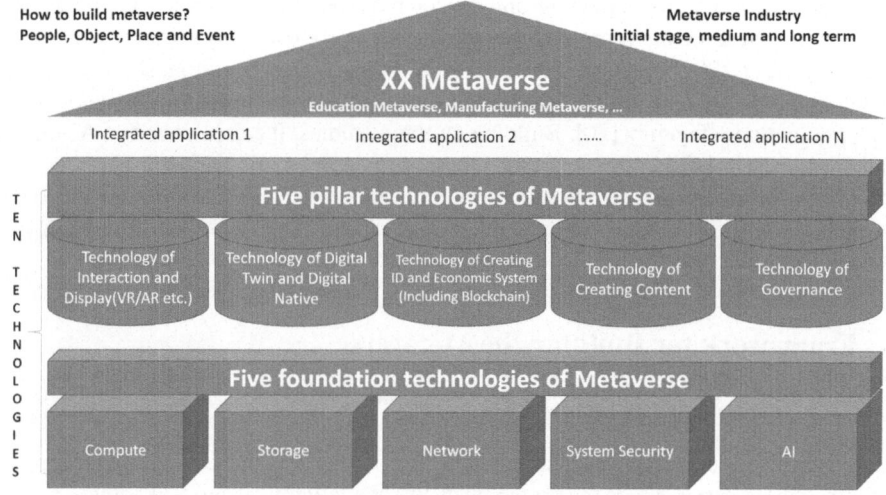

Fig. 1. The Ten Major Technologies of the Metaverse

3.2 The Five Foundations of Metaverse

Human development requires energy sources like coal, oil, and natural gas. Similarly, the Metaverse, a world connecting the virtual and physical, needs "energy" input, just as Earth needs sunlight. This "energy" is the continuous computing power supplied by our real world. Computing power supports the operation and development of digital humans and their virtual society, as well as their thinking and decision-making. Here, computing power includes computing, storage, network, security, and AI capabilities, in the broadest sense. Generally, computing power refers to the computing power of CPUs (central processing units) or AI computing power of GPUs (graphics processing units).

3.3   The Five Pillars of Metaverse

If the foundation of the Metaverse (the energy cornerstone, which is the computing power input system from the physical world) is already built, how can we create an exciting new digital world? Initially, this digital world is a desert and needs people, objects, scenes, and events.

People from the physical world use interactive and display technologies to manage the lives and work of digital humans.

Digital twin technology maps objects, scenes, and events from the physical world into the Metaverse, quickly constructing a familiar environment for digital humans. Digital native technology allows for imaginative spaces different from the physical world, such as teleportation and explosive hairstyles.

Digital humans need an "ID" and a "wallet" to navigate and explore the digital world, which requires the pre-creation of identity and economic systems.

People desire rich experiences, and digital humans need exciting applications, requiring content creation, such as 3D movies, games, social interactions, art, tourism, education, training, and scientific exploration.

As digital humans increase from a desert to villages, castles, nations, and even civilizations, consensus, rules, and even laws within the Metaverse are indispensable, known as governance technologies.

3.4   Integrated Applications and the Metaverse in Various Industries

Building on the foundational technologies of the Metaverse, particularly digital twin and AI technologies, the AI-powered clothing customization system exemplifies how these innovations can be practically applied to bridge the virtual and physical worlds. This system leverages the integration of digital twins and artificial intelligence to revolutionize the customization and production of clothing within the Metaverse.

By automating the design and fitting process, this system not only improves efficiency but also offers an unprecedented level of customization, which was previously unattainable with traditional methods. This innovation allows users to engage with the Metaverse in a more meaningful way, participating in the creation of their own clothing and experiencing a seamless integration of digital and physical realities. The system's ability to translate virtual designs into physical products highlights the transformative potential of the Metaverse in redefining consumer-producer interactions.

Integrated applications, such as digital humans, or hosting Metaverse fashion weeks in Decentraland, and Metaverse applications in various industries, create new business models and user experiences by integrating two or more of the aforementioned Metaverse technologies. For example:

1) Education Metaverse: The education Metaverse uses VR and AR technologies to create virtual classrooms and laboratories, allowing students to learn in an immersive

environment. Digital twin technology can simulate various experimental scenarios, while AI technology is used for personalized learning and real-time feedback. For instance, through virtual reality, students can conduct remote field trips, participate in simulated experiments, and interact with virtual tutors for immediate guidance.

2) Industrial Metaverse: The industrial Metaverse uses digital twin technology to create virtual factories and production lines for real-time monitoring and optimization of actual production processes. Combining AI and IoT technologies enables predictive maintenance and intelligent manufacturing. Enterprises can conduct equipment debugging, process optimization, and employee training in a virtual environment, reducing costs and increasing efficiency. For example, BMW uses NVIDIA's Omniverse platform to create virtual factories for 1:1 real-time simulation [21]. Also we will introduce AI-powered clothing customization system later.

3) Cultural and Tourism Metaverse: The cultural and tourism Metaverse uses VR and AR technologies to provide tourists with immersive travel experiences. Digital twin technology can recreate historical sites and cultural landscapes, allowing users to explore famous attractions worldwide with virtual guides. Additionally, users can participate in cultural activities and experiences in the virtual world, enhancing the interactivity and engagement of tourism. For example, the virtual version of Disneyland allows visitors to experience various amusement projects and performances online.

4) Urban Metaverse: The urban Metaverse uses digital twin technology and IoT to create a virtual version of a wise city, achieving digital and intelligent city management. Through real-time data analysis and AI technology, city managers can optimize traffic flow, energy consumption, and public services. Citizens can participate in urban planning and community activities through a virtual platform, improving the quality of urban life and management efficiency.

4   Practical Application in the Metaverse

4.1   Overview of AI-Driven Digital Twin-Based Clothing Customization System

The Metaverse, a virtual realm that seamlessly integrates with the physical world, represents a groundbreaking evolution in how we interact with technology and digital content. In this digital world, applications are not only about entertainment and social interaction but extend to practical and commercial uses that enhance user experience and drive new business models. A prime example of this is the AI-driven digital twin-based clothing customization system. This system leverages the convergence of AI and digital twin technology to create personalized and immersive shopping experiences. By generating 3D clothing models based solely on two photographs and the user's height data, the system eliminates the need for in-person measurements for tailoring. Users can remotely design and customize well-fitting, personalized garments. For instance, Chinese individuals residing in Western countries can design and customize unique cheongsams remotely (Fig. 2).

Shortly after the launch of the clothing customization system, virtual fitting rooms will be introduced, allowing users to try on garments in a simulated environment, this system exemplifies the integration of virtual and physical realms, addressing the challenge

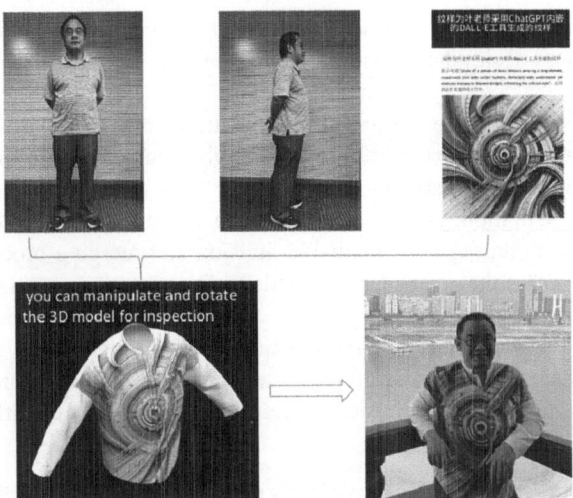

Fig. 2. The process of AI-driven digital twin-based clothing customization system

of bridging the two, exemplifying the Metaverse's potential to transform industries. This chapter will explore this system as a practical case study, demonstrating how such innovations embody the Metaverse's principles of co-creation, co-governance, and shared benefits.

4.2 Technical Framework and Operation of Clothing Customization System

The AI-driven system transforms 2D images into precise 3D models. This allows users to virtually try on garments with high accuracy.

In the digital two-dimensional (2D) segmentation method for garment pattern pieces, the existing two main triangulation algorithms—incremental algorithm and divide-and-conquer algorithm as picture below (Fig. 3).

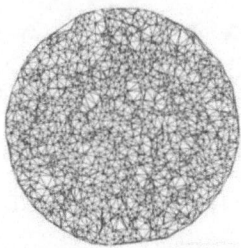

Fig. 3. Traditional Triangulation Algorithm in Garment Pattern Cutting

They have the following significant drawbacks:

1. High Computational Load: These algorithms require extensive calculations when processing large-scale data, leading to prolonged computation times and low efficiency.
2. Low Accuracy: Due to the presence of cumulative errors within the algorithms, the final triangulation results often fail to meet high accuracy requirements, especially when handling complex garment shapes.
3. Cumulative Calculation Errors: Particularly in the divide-and-conquer algorithm, errors accumulate during each recursive division and merging process, which progressively increases the error margin, resulting in a significant deviation in the final output.
4. Poor Integration with Fabric Characteristics: Existing algorithms struggle to adequately consider the warp and weft characteristics of the fabric, resulting in triangulations that do not match the physical properties of the fabric well, affecting the fit of the garment.

To overcome these drawbacks, the AI-driven clothing customization system proposes an improved digital 2D segmentation method for garment pattern pieces as picture below (Fig. 4).

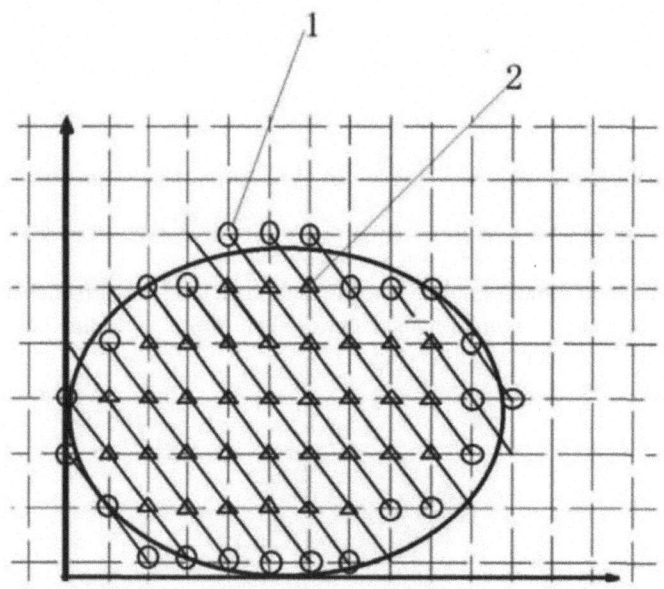

Fig. 4. Adaptive grid and precise positioning 2D segmentation diagram

The method includes the following steps:

1. Adaptive Meshing and High-Precision Sampling: By obtaining the 2D shape and estimated density of the garment pattern piece, adaptive meshing technology is utilized

to dynamically adjust the mesh precision, especially in edge areas where higher sampling precision is applied to ensure the accuracy of edge segmentation points. This approach improves segmentation accuracy and reduces computational complexity.

2. Enhanced Triangulation Point Selection Algorithm: When selecting triangulation points, a combination of optimized algorithms such as the Green-Sibson algorithm, Bowyer algorithm, and Lawson algorithm is used. Initially, all edge segmentation points are identified, and then internal triangulation points are selected through iterative optimization. During this process, the system automatically detects the matching conditions between mesh nodes and garment scatter points, prioritizing the most suitable mesh nodes, thereby reducing errors. The enhanced triangulation algorithm plays a critical role in achieving high-precision cutting for complex garment shapes, thereby improving the fit and quality of the final product.

3. Efficient Mesh Line Connection Method: By optimizing the mesh line connection strategy, the diagonals of adjacent meshes are crossed to form a more stable and regular triangulation structure. This method not only ensures the accuracy of the segmentation results but also greatly improves computational efficiency.

4. Precise Positioning with Coordinate System: To ensure accurate positioning of the pattern pieces in the 2D plane, a 2D coordinate system is established so that the leftmost edge of the pattern piece is tangent to the Y-axis of the coordinate system. By combining the precise mesh lines of the coordinate system, accurate digital segmentation of the pattern pieces is achieved. This step greatly enhances the ability to handle complex garment shapes.

Through these improved technical solutions, the method demonstrates significant advantages in the following areas:

1. Accuracy Enhancement: Compared to existing algorithms, this method offers higher segmentation accuracy, capable of handling complex pattern shapes with a precision requirement of up to 0.5 mm, while also reducing cumulative calculation errors.

2. Increased Computational Efficiency: The optimized algorithm reduces unnecessary computational steps, significantly improving computational efficiency, making it suitable for high-precision segmentation on personal computers and other low-configuration hardware.

3. Reduced System Errors: The use of high-precision algorithms and adaptive meshing technology greatly reduces system errors, ensuring the accuracy and consistency of each segmentation.

4. Better Integration with Fabric Characteristics: The improved algorithm better integrates with the warp and weft characteristics of the fabric, resulting in triangulations that more accurately match the physical properties of the fabric, enhancing garment fit.

This precise mapping allows for realistic garment fitting, where users can interact with the system through AR and VR interfaces, experiencing the garment in a fully immersive environment. Additionally, the system supports real-time adjustments and provides immediate feedback, making the virtual try-on process intuitive and user-friendly. Users can easily transform their favorite designs, artworks, or any graphical patterns into NFTs, which can then be converted into physical garments. This framework not only enhances the user experience but also sets the stage for future integration with blockchain-based technologies, enabling users to own, trade, and wear digital versions of their customized clothing.

This precise mapping allows for realistic garment fitting, where users can interact with the system through AR and VR interfaces, experiencing the garment in a fully immersive environment. Additionally, the system supports real-time adjustments and provides immediate feedback, making the virtual try-on process intuitive and user-friendly. Users can easily transform their favorite designs, artworks, or any graphical patterns into NFTs, which can then be converted into physical garments. This framework not only enhances the user experience but also sets the stage for future integration with block-chain-based technologies, enabling users to own, trade, and wear digital versions of their customized clothing.

4.3 Implications and Future Directions in the Metaverse

The implementation of the AI-driven digital twin-based clothing customization system within the Metaverse has far-reaching implications for both consumers and the fashion industry. While the Metaverse offers numerous opportunities, it also poses significant challenges, particularly in terms of data privacy, security, and the ethical use of AI and digital twin technologies. Addressing these concerns is crucial for sustainable development and user trust.

By providing a highly personalized shopping experience, this system meets the growing demand for customized products and services, reflecting a shift towards consumer-centric business models. Moreover, the integration of such technology within the Metaverse highlights the potential for creating new economic opportunities, such as virtual fashion shows, digital clothing lines, and even the development of a new marketplace for virtual goods. Looking forward, the system is poised to evolve with advancements in AI and digital twin technologies, offering even more sophisticated and realistic simulations. Future challenges include ensuring data privacy and security, optimizing the user interface for broader accessibility, and exploring the commercial viability of integrating NFTs and other blockchain-based assets. These directions will not only influence the future of fashion within the Metaverse but could also set a precedent for how other industries adapt to this emerging digital landscape [22]. Future research will focus on enhancing the integration of blockchain technologies with digital twins to enable secure and scalable solutions within the Metaverse. Additionally, exploring the role of AI in creating more adaptive and personalized user experiences will be key to the Metaverse's continued evolution.

5 Summary

In summary, the Metaverse represents a multidimensional co-creative mutual trust network, integrating virtual and physical worlds through advanced technologies. Leveraging the five pillars—interactive and display technologies, digital twin and digital native technologies, identity and economic systems, content creation, and governance technologies—along with the five foundations—AI, network, computing, storage, and security technologies—the Metaverse offers an expansive, immersive, and interactive platform.

The integration of these technologies facilitates new user experiences, transforming industries such as fashion, education, and manufacturing. A notable example is the AI-driven digital twin-based clothing customization system, which bridges the gap between digital design and physical production. By allowing users to generate 3D models of clothing from photos, the system demonstrates the potential for personalized virtual commerce, redefining the relationship between consumers and producers.

Beyond fashion, the Metaverse enables significant innovations across sectors, such as virtual classrooms in education and smart factories in manufacturing. As these applications grow, the Metaverse is poised to become a vital space for collaboration, creativity, and commerce. However, challenges related to data privacy, security, and governance must be addressed to ensure the sustainable and ethical growth of this digital ecosystem.

Looking ahead, the future of the Metaverse will be shaped by advancements in AI, digital twins, and blockchain, offering even more sophisticated, real-time interactions and personalized experiences. This evolution will redefine how people live, work, and interact in the digital and physical worlds.

References

1. Fan, Y., Huang, T., Meng, Y., Cheng, S.: The current opportunities and challenges of Web 3.0. arXiv:2306.03351 (2023)
2. Acceleration Studies Foundation: Metaverse Roadmap: Pathways to the 3D Web, pp. 1–28 (2007). https://www.w3.org/2008/WebVideo/Annotations/wiki/images/1/19/Metaverse RoadmapOverview.pdf
3. Matthew, B.: The Metaverse: What It Is, Where to Find It, and Who Will Build It (2020). https://www.matthewball.co/all/themetaverse
4. Ye, Y.: Ten technologies of metaverse, pp. 99–110. Translation and Publishing House, China (2022). ISBN 978-7-5001-7112-6
5. Schroeder, R.: Defining virtual worlds and virtual environments. J. Virtual Reality 12(3), 133–141 (2008)

6. Dionisio, J.D.N., Burns, W.G., III., Gilbert, R.: 3D virtual worlds and the metaverse: current status and future possibilities. ACM Comput. Surv. (CSUR) **45**(3), 34 (2013)

7. Lee, L.-H., et al.: All one needs to know about metaverse: a complete survey on technological singularity, virtual ecosystem, and research agenda. J. IEEE Access **9**, 148191–148243 (2021)

8. Park, S.M., Kim, Y.G.: A metaverse: taxonomy, components, applications, and open challenges. J. Inf. Process. Syst. **18**(1), 1–12 (2022)

9. Gartner.: Top Strategic Technology Trends for 2022. Gartner Research Report (2022)

10. Ratan, R., Hasler, B.S.: Presence in virtual reality: theories, measurements, and emerging research topics. Virtual Reality **25**(1), 1–15 (2021)

11. Swan, M.: Blockchain: Blueprint for a New Economy. O'Reilly Media (2015)

12. Wüst, K., Gervais, A.: Do you need a Blockchain? In: Proceedings of the 2018 Crypto Valley Conference on Blockchain Technology (CVCBT), pp. 45–54 (2018)

13. Kim, Y., Kim, H.: Tokenomics in the metaverse: a case study of sandbox and decentraland. J. Blockchain Res. **3**(2), 150–165 (2021)

14. Hsieh, Y.H., Wu, T.Y., Wang, C.S.: Blockchain, governance, and user engagement in decentralized virtual worlds. J. Virtual Environ. **10**(1), 22–36 (2022)

15. Xu, D., Zhou, P., Lin, Z., Kim, H.: Scalability and Interoperability in blockchain-based metaverse applications. J. Distrib. Ledger Technol. **14**(3), 25–38 (2022)

16. Grieves, M.: Digital Twin: Manufacturing Excellence through Virtual Factory Replication. Digital Twin White Paper (2014)

17. Tao, F., Zhang, H., Liu, A., Nee, A.Y.C.: Digital twin in industry: state-of-the-art. IEEE Trans. Industr. Inf. **15**(4), 2405–2415 (2018)

18. Qi, Q., Tao, F.: Digital twin and big data towards smart manufacturing and industry 4.0: 360 degree comparison. IEEE Access **7**, 102965–102979 (2019)

19. Boschert, S., Rosen, R.: Digital twin—the simulation aspect. In: Hehenberger, P., Bradley, D. (eds.) Mechatronic Futures, pp. 59–74. Springer (2016). https://doi.org/10.1007/978-3-319-32156-1_5

20. Kritzinger, W., Karner, M., Traar, G., Henjes, J., Sihn, W.: Digital twin in manufacturing: a categorical literature review and classification. IFAC-PapersOnLine **52**(13), 1016–1022 (2020)

21. Spatial Reality: How BMW Uses NVIDIA Omniverse for a 30% Increase in Production Planning Efficiency, pp. 1–3 (2021). https://spatialreality.io/how-bmw-uses-nvidia-omniverse-for-a-30-increase-in-production-planning-efficiency/

22. Madanchian, M., Taherdoost, H.: Business Model Evolution in the Age of NFTs

Short Paper Track

SRv6 Metaverse – Architecture for Virtual Worlds

Michael McBride[1]($\boxtimes$), Keyi Zhou[2], Zhenbin Li[2], Tianran Zhou[2], and Shuping Peng[2]

[1] Futurewei, Los Angeles, USA
mmcbride@futurewei.com
[2] Huawei, Beijing, China
{zhukeyi,lizhenbin,zhoutianran,pengshuping}@huawei.com

Abstract. A metaverse provides an immersive and linked experience for individuals. Experiences will be enabled by VR headsets, gaming systems, desktop computers, smartphones, etc., while there will likely emerge several metaverses which in turn will need interconnection. A metaverse may be portrayed as a platform that utilizes networking to build an open ecosystem in which different platforms co-exist to serve all users. The emergence of a metaverse as a virtual environment encompassing augmented reality, virtual reality, and the Internet is reshaping the way we interact, communicate, and transact. As the infrastructure supporting a metaverse becomes increasingly critical, the choice of interdomain networking technologies becomes pivotal. This paper explores the advantages of Segment Routing IPv6 (SRv6) over other technologies, particularly Multiprotocol Label Switching (MPLS), in building robust and scalable networks for a metaverse. By examining key features and requirements of a metaverse, we illustrate why SRv6 presents a superior choice for delivering immersive interdomain experiences and supporting diverse applications. We will show that MPLS will gradually be replaced by SRv6 on existing IP transport networks in order to support new metaverse application requirements.

Keywords: Metaverse · SRv6 · BGP · MPLS · Security

1 Introduction

The promise of a metaverse is to link together a variety of virtual experiences, including gaming, property, art, music, sports, etc., and consumed within and between worlds. The concept of a metaverse, as envisioned by science fiction, and now increasingly realized through technological advancements, represents a virtual universe where individuals can interact with each other and digital objects in real-time. This immersive environment requires a robust interdomain networking infrastructure capable of supporting very high-bandwidth, low- latency communication across diverse devices and platforms. In this context, the choice of networking protocols plays a crucial role in ensuring seamless connectivity and optimal, traffic engineered, performance. This paper presents SRv6 as the best protocol to deliver on the requirements of a metaverse and compares SRv6 and MPLS in the context of building the most optimum networking infrastructure.

© The Author(s), under exclusive license to Springer Nature Switzerland AG 2025
C. Xing et al. (Eds.): METAVERSE 2024, LNCS 15429, pp. 97–102, 2025.
https://doi.org/10.1007/978-3-031-76977-1_7

One such key metaverse function is to ensure the large-scale network connectivity within, and beyond, wall gardens that is being envisioned as key for a metaverse. As a consequence, BGP, which is the protocol of the Internet, is likely at the heart of any future metaverse development and rollout. This can be observed already in early developments, e.g., of Microsoft's network architecture for the large Meta, which already uses BGP for Internet wide network connectivity and will likely continue to do so.

As explained in [1] Segment Routing IPv6 (SRv6) is a new network architecture that leverages IPv6 data plane encapsulation to enable flexible and efficient traffic engineering. It allows for the creation of explicit paths through the network by encoding routing instructions directly into packet headers. MPLS, on the other hand, is a widely adopted protocol for traffic engineering and label switching in packet-switched networks. It operates by assigning labels to packets at the ingress router and using these labels to forward packets along predetermined paths through the network.

To effectively support the diverse requirements of a metaverse, the underlying networking infrastructure must possess several key attributes:

1) Low Latency: Real-time interaction within a metaverse necessitates minimal latency to ensure a seamless user experience.
2) Scalability: The network should be able to accommodate a large number of concurrent users and devices without sacrificing performance.
3) Flexibility: As a metaverse evolves, the networking infrastructure must be adaptable to support new applications and services.
4) Security: With sensitive data and transactions occurring, within a metaverse, robust security mechanisms are essential to protect against threats and breaches.
5) Simplified Operations: Streamlined network operations and management are crucial for maintaining uptime and resolving issues promptly.
6) High Throughput: A very large amount of data will be generated by various metaverse components. And this data will need to captured for real time analysis. The network will need to support high throughput and capture rates.
7) Power Efficiency: The computing power needed, in a data center, to process and store the metaverse data will be immense. The computing capacity will need to be built in the most power efficient, environmentally friendly (green) way possible.

Our contribution in this paper is to outline how SRv6 is the ideal system to provide simple and flexible metaverse interconnection. We provide an overview of MPLS, an overview of SRv6 and then show how SRv6 is the best protocol to meet many of these key attributes and to carry interdomain metaverse into the future.

2 MPLS for Metaverse

MPLS was first developed in the 1990's and continues to be an important networking solution for many businesses and commonly found in service provider networks today. Before MPLS, there were several networking protocols in use including Frame Relay and ATM. MPLS introduced a powerful solution which provided separation of control and data planes and the subsequent ability to override routing decisions based on policies and labels. MPLS provides good QoS guarantees for IP connection-oriented label forwarding and supports Traffic Engineering (TE), Virtual Private Networks (VPN), and Fast Reroute (FRR). The success of MPLS, particularly in service provider networks, is based largely on these TE, VPN and FRR capabilities.

Because IP networks are cost-effective and MPLS provides good TE, VPN and FRR capabilities, IP/MPLS networks gradually replaced dedicated networks such as ATM and Frame-Relay.

MPLS, however, complicates inter-domain network interconnection by causing isolated network islands. Many services require E2E deployment including over multiple MPLS domains. MPLS requires complex inter-domain MPLS solutions. RFC4364 [2] specifies protocol and procedures for BGP/MPLS IP Virtual Private Networks (VPNs), including different options (A/B/C) of Inter-AS support. It has been difficult for service providers to deploy services across MPLS do-mains. To achieve cross-domain deployment, service providers need to use traditional inter-AS MPLS VPN technologies which are complex and slow down service provisioning.

Scalability and extensibility are two other aspects of MPLS that may prove less than ideal for interdomain metaverse solutions. In the MPLS label space, for instance, there are 20 bits for the MPLS label. As the network scale expands, the label space is no longer sufficient. Additionally, the control plane of MPLS networks face complexity and scalability challenges. Scalability is limited when MPLS is used in cross-domain scenarios because MPLS labels don't contain reachability information. They instead must be bound to routable IP addresses and the binding must be propagated across domains. We will show that SRv6 makes cross-domain deployment much easier.

Another complexity of using MPLS is that all devices along an MPLS path have to maintain the mappings between labels and Forwarding Equivalence Classes (FECs). Even when transitioning from MPLS to SR-MPLS (Segment Routing MPLS) the existing network needs to undergo significant changes in the initial migration steps which will take a fair amount of time. We will show later how SRv6 allows the existing network to be upgraded on demand and only certain devices need to be upgraded.

Lastly, MPLS Traffic Engineering (MPLS-TE) uses RSVP- TE as it's signaling protocol. RSVP-TE needs to maintain the per-flow path states on each node along a path. As the network scale increases, so does the workload for RSVP- TE to maintain the path states, consuming excessive device resources. As a result, it is difficult to deploy RSVP-TE on large-scale networks such as interdomain metaverse.

3 SRv6 for Metaverse

MPLS was first developed in the 1990's and continues to be an important networking solution for many businesses and commonly found in service provider networks today.

Segment Routing (RFC8402 [3]) brings a powerful way to introduce source routing into modern networks running either MPLS or IPv6 data planes. Segment Routing is a source routing paradigm which can program the forwarding path of packets by allowing the ingress of the path to insert forwarding instructions into packets. A segment is an instruction which is executed on a node for packet processing. There are various reasons why SRv6 is the ideal solution for interdomain metaverse deployments.

1) *SRv6 is based on IPv6:* Metaverse solutions need to be deployed using IPv6 only. One of the biggest IPv4 problems is its insufficient address resources. The Internet Assigned Numbers Authority (IANA) announced, in 2011, that the last IPv4 address blocks were allocated. There are no more IPv4 address blocks. Network Address Translation (NAT) has been used to help alleviate the address depletion by reusing private network address blocks but most would agree that is not the long-term solution and is certainly not what a metaverse wants to utilize as it complicates network deployment. It is also difficult for IPv4 networks to support new services which require header extensions such as Source Routing (SR), Service Function Chaining (SFC) and In-band Operations, Administration and Maintenance (IOAM). Insufficient extensibility of the IPv4 header constrains further IPv4 development.

  IPv6, on the other hand, solves the problems of limited address space and insufficient extensibility. IPv6 increases the address space from 32 bits to 128 bits. IPv6 also has an extension header mechanism. RFC8200 [4] defines various extension headers which provide good extensibility and programmability. SRv6 is based only on IPv6 which is preferred for metaverse deployment particularly for extensibility of IPv6. The Segment Routing header (SRH) is an extension header added to IPv6 packets to implement SRv6 based on the IPv6 forwarding plane.

2) *SRv6 provides network programmability for the Metaverse:* Segment Routing based on MPLS (SR-MPLS) can provide good programmability but it can't satisfy services that need to carry metadata, such as SFC and IOAM. MPLS encapsulation has relatively poor extensibility. Compared with SR-MPLS, SRv6, which is based on IPv6 data plane, provides better extensibility.

  A metaverse needs to have a global network view and the ability to visualize traffic capability in order to make optimal decisions from a global perspective of the network or respond to traffic engineering requirements. Software Defined Networking (SDN) provides a network abstraction for users to manage networks and is also expected to be a key architecture of a metaverse.

3) *SRv6 simplifies the network:* SRv6 is compatible with IPv6 forwarding and can implement interconnection of different network domains easily through IPv6 reachability. The native IP attribute of SRv6 greatly simplifies basic transport technologies. SDN can be gradually rolled out on service provider networks in a simple to complex manner. In SRv6, label distribution protocols, such as RSVP-TE, are not needed.

  SRv6 enables the programming of metaverse services and transport networks based on a single data plane. Only IGP (ISIS, OSPF) and BGP extensions are required in the SRv6 control plane, thereby reducing the number of control plane protocols. ISIS and OSPF have been extended to carry SRv6 information, which in turn makes it possible to implement SRv6 control plane functions while also avoiding the need to maintain certain control plane protocols, such as RSVP-TE and LDP.

4) *Interdomain SRv6:* It has been difficult for service providers to deploy services across MPLS domains because they have needed to use inter-AS MPLS VPN technologies which are complex and which slow down service provisioning. Multiple Inter-AS MPLS VPN interdomain solutions have been provided, such as Option A, Option B and Option C.

  If SR-MPLS is used for interdomain, Segment ID's (SIDs) need to be imported from one domain to another in order to establish an end-to-end SR path. Segment

Routing Global Blocks (SRGBs) and node SIDs must be planned network wide to avoid SID conflicts.

Because MPLS labels don't contain reachability information, they must be bound to routable IP addresses and the binding must be propagated across domains. On large-scale networks, numerous MPLS entries need to be generated on border nodes which places a heavy burden on the control and forwarding planes.

SRv6 makes interdomain deployment easy as it supports native IPv6 and can work purely based on IPv6 reachability. SRv6 L3VPN services, for instance, can be deployed across domains by importing IPv6 routes from one domain to another through BGP. This significantly simplifies service deployment.

5) *Kernel level SRv6 support:* SRv6 is available in the mainstream Linux kernel (since version 4.10). As such, performance, security and stability are increased for SRv6 users and applications. With SRv6, a metaverse can naturally start from the applications themselves and not the network devices.

Service Providers need to provide fine-granularity and application level SLA guarantees for better Quality of Experience (QoE) for users. Online gaming, video streaming, video conferencing and now metaverse have demanding requirements of the network. Adding application awareness to the network layer helps enable the fine granularity application requirements. The programmability provided by IPv6 can be used to convey information about applications.

Application Aware Networking (APN) aims to deliver application awareness to the new services (such as metaverse). APN conveys application information in the network data plane to allow for fine grain requirements to be specified to the network. APN6 makes use of IPv6 extension headers to convey application related information along with the packet to facilitate service deployment and SLA guarantees.

APN IDs are used to identify applications so that traffic can be steered into SRv6 paths in order to achieve application traffic division and flexible path selection. Network nodes can steer application packets to the matched SRv6 policy. The network can use ID's, carried in APN6 packet headers, to identify high-priority service flows and steer them into an SLA-compliant SRv6 path, guaranteeing low delay, for instance.

6) *SRv6 Multicast:* Live events, such as sports and concerts, are an important element in a metaverse. IP Multicast, or P2MP communication, is an important set of networking protocols to ensure bandwidth saving when delivering these live events to large audience simultaneously. Bandwidth savings will be crucial in very high bandwidth metaverse deployments. Traditional multicast solutions, deployed largely today, request multicast tree building using the control plane and maintain end to end tree state per flow. SRv6, on the other hand, reduces the state of intermediate nodes by indicating forwarding behaviors in the ingress nodes near the service source. This greatly simplifies deployment and maintenance.

Bit Index Explicit Replication IPv6 (BIERv6) encapsulation simplifies the control plane protocols and allows the network programming by the ingress to steer multicast packets to multiple destination nodes. Combined with SRv6, BIERv6 allows both unicast and multicast services to be implemented based on the unified IPv6 data plane and the unified IGP/BGP control plane.

On a converged MPLS transport network, MVPN supports MPLS encapsulation, uses the signaling extended based on the unicast LDP and RSVP-TE protocols and leverages FRR in MPLS. As networks evolve towards SRv6, the disadvantages of MPLS P2MP based MVPN are becoming more prominent:

Wasted Bandwidth: A MVPN uses a I-PMSI tunnel to carry multiple multicast flows of a VPN, wasting traffic bandwidth resources.

Increased Network Cost: A dedicated P2MP tunnel needs to be established for each multicast flow using mLDP or RSVP- TE. As the number of multicast flows increases, there is an increased need for more P2MP tunnels.

Complexity: The Multicast Distribution Tree (MDT) establishment through mLDP is complex. mLDP on the ingress PE needs to generate a tunnel ID (FEC) and advertise the FEC to each egress PE through BGP. Then, mLDP on each egress PE, searches for a route based on the root IP address in the FEC and sends an mLDP mapping message to the upstream node. The message is then forwarded hop by hop to the ingress PE to establish a P2MP MDT.

With the reachability and configurability of IPv6 addresses, BIERv6, on the other hand, can easily support inter-AS deployment. BIERv6 adapts to the development of SRv6 networks. Like SRv6, BIERv6 requires network devices to have certain hardware forwarding capabilities. Routers and switches must be programmable and capable of evolving.

4   Conclusion

Segment Routing over IPv6 (SRv6) is IP technology which helps meet the new network requirements of interdomain metaverse ecosystems. SRv6 provides comprehensive network programming capabilities to better meet the requirements of metaverse's new network services and is compatible with IPv6 to simplify network service deployment. A metaverse will need very high bandwidth networking. SRv6 traffic engineering can utilize network bandwidth more effectively than traditional MPLS RSVP-TE. The more immersive the metaverse, the more bandwidth will be needed. SRv6's increased ability to support new technologies, such as AI and blockchain, through network programmability, will be required.

SRv6 is the best solution for interdomain metaverse deployment due to its ability to leverage the existing IPv6 infrastructure and routing protocols. SRv6 greatly simplifies the network (particularly vs MPLS) and yet provides complex programmability that will be required by a variety of metaverse applications.

References

1. Li, Z., Hu, Z., Li, C.: in Srv6 Network Programming (2021)
2. Rosen, E., Rekhter, Y.: in BGP/MPLS IP Virtual Private Networks (VPNs) (2006)
3. Filsfils, C., Previdi, S., Ginsberg, L., Decraene, B., Litkowski, S., Shakir, R.: in Segment Routing Architecture (2018)
4. Deering, S., Hinden, R.: in Internet Protocol, Version 6 (IPv6) Specification (2017)

AI-Enabled Metaverse for Education: Challenges and Opportunities

Yuling Chen[1], Ningyu Fan[2(✉)], and Hongyang Wu[1]

[1] Ningbo University of Finance and Economics, Ningbo 315175, China
chenyuling@nbufe.edu.cn, 2222450074@s.nbufe.edu.cn
[2] Huazhong University of Science and Technology, Wuhan 430074, China
fanningyu@hust.edu.cn

Abstract. The Metaverse is a virtual, interactive space parallel to the real world, offering an immersive experience with seamless connectivity. The combination of Metaverse and artificial intelligence provides new infinite potentials for education. The AI-enabled Metaverse has distinct characteristics such as personalized learning paths, automated content creation, and adaptive assessment, etc. These new features provide opportunities to achieve the goals of smart education through applications on class-based instruction, group-based learning, individual-based learning, and autonomous learning processes. However, the implementation still faces the challenges from technological accessibility, data privacy problem, pedagogical integration, sustainability, disruption of use, and ethical considerations. While the improvement of emerging Metaverse devices and widespread of Metaverse applications bring opportunities to satisfy diverse educational needs, it is necessary to further take a holistic approach to build a complete AI-enabled educational Metaverse ecosystem, which requires multi-dimensional support from the perspectives of techniques, policies, and value.

Keywords: Metaverse · Artificial Intelligence · Education

1 Introduction

The Metaverse is an immersive and interactive three-dimensional virtual world built with advanced technologies such as virtual reality, augmented reality, and artificial intelligence [1]. The Metaverse has created a new dimension for interactive and immersive learning and is rapidly becoming an integral part of modern education [2]. The application of the Metaverse in education is characterized by realism, personalization, high interactivity, cross-temporal capabilities, and diverse visualization [3].

The introduction of the AI-powered Metaverse, especially with the integration of Large Language Models (LLM) [4] and AI-Generated Content (AIGC) [5], has brought new power to the field of education. For example, LLMs analyze vast amounts of student data to generate tailored lesson plans, ensuring that each student receives content that aligns with their learning style and progress. AIGC can generate interactive quizzes, games, and scenarios that adapt to the student's progress.

C. Xing et al. (Eds.): METAVERSE 2024, LNCS 15429, pp. 103–113, 2025.
https://doi.org/10.1007/978-3-031-76977-1_8

However, existing research primarily focuses on technical optimizations within specific scenarios, neglecting a systematic summation and analysis of the new characteristics exhibited by these contemporary applications [6]. Presently, the exploration of AI-driven educational Metaverse applications remains in its nascent stage. Therefore, a comprehensive analysis of both existing research and practical applications, aimed at identifying future opportunities and challenges, appears to be particularly crucial and urgent. Such an analysis holds significant potential to propel the better development and implementation of the AI Metaverse for education.

This paper proposes a systematic review on the research and applications of AI-enabled Metaverse in education. We first introduce the fundamental technologies, and then identify the new and distinct features of AI-powered Metaverse for the goals of smart education, such as the abilities of enhanced personalization, interactive and adaptive learning, and diverse content creation, etc. Finally, we conclude most concerned challenges and opportunities, and propose possible paths to better education.

2 The Basic Technologies of AI-Enabled Metaverse

The Metaverse is a convergence of multiple cutting-edge technologies, each playing a vital role in its functioning and user experience. This section briefly introduces the preliminaries of Metaverse technologies.

Digital Twins (DTs). Digital Twin technology refers to the utilization of physical models, sensors, operational history, and other data to create a mapping of physical equipment in a virtual space, reflecting its entire lifecycle process [7]. The characteristics of Digital Twin technologies include close correlation between virtual and physical entities, real-time monitoring, and powerful data analysis abilities.

Spatial Computing. It refers to the use of spatial data and spatial relationships in computational processes [8]. Emerging related technologies include Virtual Reality (VR), Augmented Reality (AR), Mixed Reality (MR), and Extended Reality (XR). These techniques utilize multiple technical means to provide users with an immersive experience that seamlessly transitions between the virtual and real worlds.

Cloud/Edge Computing. In the Metaverse, cloud computing technology facilitates real-time image rendering, physical simulations, and other computationally intensive tasks. Edge computing brings computing resources closer to data sources, improving the overall performance of Metaverse [9].

Web 3.0. As a key technology in the Metaverse, it combines decentralization, token economics, and blockchain technology to create a more secure, democratic, and efficient digital environment [10]. Web 3.0 is also designed to integrate seamlessly with other emerging technologies like AR/VR, AI, and the Metaverse itself.

Artificial Intelligence (AI). The Metaverse, as a virtual shared space, relies heavily on advanced AI technologies to enhance user experiences and enable seamless interactions [11]. Natural Language Processing (NLP) allows the Metaverse to understand and analyze human language, enabling features like smart chatbots, voice assistants, and intelligent search engines. Computer Vision (CV) techniques, such as object recognition and tracking, are used in the Metaverse to identify and interact with virtual objects, avatars, and environments. Generative models, such as Generative Adversarial Networks (GANs), can create new content based on existing data. With the development of Large Language Models (LLMs) and Artificial Intelligence Generated Content (AIGC), AI-driven Metaverse has become a trend in practical uses.

Discussion. In the era of AI-enhanced society, the basic AI models and algorithms are closely integrated into other computer technologies either for improving the efficiency of original functions or for creating new experience. This paper focuses more on the distinct functions of the educational Metaverse brought by AI.

3 Applications of AI-Enabled Metaverse in Education

The functions of AI-enabled Metaverse in education are first introduced in this section. The applications for smart educations are then illustrated from four levels.

3.1 Distinct Functions of AI-Enabled Metaverse in Education

In the Metaverse, AI assistance makes learning more efficient and personalized. This integration diversifies educational formats as shown in Fig. 1.

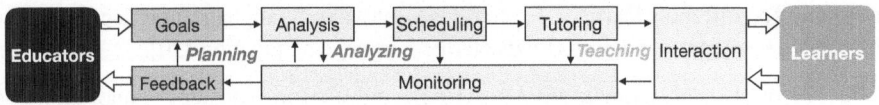

Fig. 1. The Workflow of AI-enabled Metaverse in Education

Planning Stage

Real-Time Feedback. AI systems provide instant feedback on student work, allowing for timely corrections and improvements [12]. LLMs can grade assignments and offer detailed feedback, enabling students to understand their mistakes immediately.

Data-Driven Insights for Educators. AI systems collect and analyze vast amounts of data on student performance, providing educators with deep insights into learning patterns, challenges, and areas of improvement [13]. This information enables educators to make informed decisions and tailor their teaching strategies accordingly.

Adaptive Assessment. LLMs can generate adaptive assessments and exam preparations based on students' performance and progress. These systems identify areas where students need improvement and provide targeted practice and feedback to help them excel in exams [14].

Analyzing Stage

Personalized Learning Paths. LLMs analyze students' learning patterns and progress to generate personalized learning paths [15]. These models adapt content and pace based on individual student's needs, ensuring an optimal learning experience tailored to their unique capabilities and interests.

Automated Content Creation. AIGC technology generates educational content dynamically, adapting to the specific needs and interests of students. This capability significantly reduces the time and effort required to create relevant and engaging educational materials [16].

Emotional Intelligence and Well-Being Monitoring. Advanced AI systems detect and analyze students' emotional states through interactions with the learning platform [17]. This capability enables timely interventions and support to promote student well-being and enhance the learning experience.

Continuous Learning and Improvement. LLMs and AIGC technologies are capable of continuous learning, adapting to the evolving needs of students and educators. These systems continuously update their knowledge base and improve their performance to provide the most relevant and up-to-date contents and methods [18].

Teaching Stage

Intelligent Tutoring Systems. AIGC creates virtual tutors that interact with students, answering questions and providing guidance [19]. These systems simulate human tutors, offering personalized attention and support to enhance the learning process.

Language Learning Enhancement. LLMs excel in language processing, making them invaluable for different learners. It provides context-rich language practice, real-time feedback, and recommendations to accelerate language acquisition [20].

Collaborative Learning Environments. AI-powered platforms foster collaboration and teamwork among students [21]. These environments facilitate group projects, discussions, and knowledge sharing, enhancing critical thinking, problem-solving, and communication skills.

Virtual Laboratories and Simulations. AIGC technology creates immersive virtual laboratories and simulations, allowing students to conduct experiments and practice skills in a safe and controlled environment [22]. These simulations provide hands-on learning experiences without the need for physical equipment or facilities.

Interactive and Engaging Educational Games. AIGC creates educational games that are both fun and educational, increasing student engagement and retention of knowledge [23]. These games utilize interactive elements and adaptive challenges to keep students engaged and learning.

Global Accessibility and Cultural Exchange. AI-powered educational tools break down geographical and cultural barriers, making high-quality education accessible to students worldwide [24]. These tools promote educational equity and facilitate cultural exchange and understanding.

Intelligent Resource Allocation. AI technology optimizes resource allocation in educational settings, ensuring that students have access to the necessary resources and support [25]. This improves the efficiency and effectiveness of educational institutions.

3.2 Applications for Smart Education

In the realm of education, smart education is defined as a student-centered educational model [26]. The advent of AI-driven Metaverse technologies intervenes at four distinct tiers, comprehensively addressing the evolving demands of smart education [27]. AI-enabled Metaverse can fulfill the goals of smart education enhanced by intelligent technologies as in the common procedure shown in Fig. 2.

Class-Based Instruction. This is a strictly guided instruction tier, where the pace of each student is synchronized by the objective of the whole class. The Metaverse usually serves as the virtual classroom and a container of knowledges, while the AI technologies can analyze the learning preference and characters of students for feedback to the teachers. In this scenario, students and teachers are closely interacted and the Metaverse is a kind of medium tools.

Group-Based Learning. Within this tier, educators provide well-defined academic objectives and direction while granting learners a moderate degree of independence in their learning journey. Learners are encouraged to investigate related subjects or pursue topics of interest, operating within the boundaries of core educational tasks with classmates. Besides the benefits in class-based instruction, the AI-enabled Metaverse can provide the students with more flexible collaborative opportunities through generated avatars. The AI system can also support more complex group analysis.

Individual-Based Learning. Educators serve as mentors and facilitators in this tier, fostering open exploration and learning experiences among learners. Learners are given considerable liberty to select research paths, devise experiments or projects, and determine their own learning timelines. This method of instruction underscores independent critical thinking and problem-solving proficiency. AI-enabled Metaverse can help break the class into individuals and provides personalized learning records for each student. There are no learning time and place limitations. Note that teachers must also be responsible to the whole learning process of each student in this scenario. AI-enabled Metaverse is trained and adjusted as a personalized encyclopedia.

Autonomous Learning. In this tier, learners enjoy substantial autonomy, formulating their own learning strategies aligned with their interests, requirements, and aspirations. Educators primarily furnish resources and assistance, whereas the direction, subject matter, and learning techniques are predominantly determined by the learners themselves. This teaching method demands exceptional levels of self-discipline and self-management from learners. In an ultra-goal, there are no teachers in this scenario through AI-enabled Metaverse. AI-agents are important in the Metaverse which can be even more attentive to detail and empathetic than human teachers.

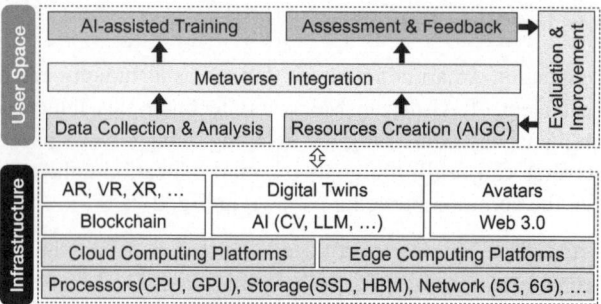

Fig. 2. AI-enabled Educational Metaverse Ecosystem

4   Challenges and Opportunities of AI-Enabled Educational Metaverse Applications

This section first introduces the challenges in AI-enabled educational Metaverse. Then, the opportunities brought by the development of AI for educations are illustrated. Finally, we propose some paths to better Metaverse for education.

4.1   Challenges

To harness the full potential of AI-enabled Metaverse in education, it is imperative to address the challenges related to accessibility, data privacy, pedagogical integration, and ethical considerations, etc.

Technological Accessibility and Infrastructure. A significant challenge is ensuring that all students have access to the necessary technology to participate in the AI-enabled Metaverse. This requires robust internet connections, powerful computing devices, and specialized software, which might not be available to everyone, especially in rural or underserved areas.

Data Privacy and Security Concerns. The collection and use of student data in the Metaverse raise significant privacy and security concerns. There is a risk of data breaches, misuse of personal information, and potential profiling or discrimination based on data analytics. Stringent data protection measures and ethical guidelines must be established to protect student privacy.

Pedagogical Integration and Teacher Training. Integrating the Metaverse into educational curricula requires a shift in teaching methodologies. Teachers need to be trained on how to effectively use AI and virtual reality tools in their classrooms. Without proper training and support, the implementation of AI-enabled Metaverse education can be challenging and may not yield the desired educational outcomes.

Cost and Sustainability. The development and maintenance of an AI-enabled Metaverse for education require significant financial investments. Schools and educational institutions may face difficulties in funding such projects, especially in resource-limited settings. Cost-effective solutions and sustainable funding models are crucial for the widespread adoption of this technology.

Technological Dependency and Disruption. Reliance on technology for education can pose risks during technical failures or disruptions. Outages or glitches in the Metaverse platform can significantly impact learning experiences, causing frustration and potential learning losses. Ensuring the reliability and stability of the technological infrastructure is essential.

Ethical Considerations and Bias. The use of AI in education raises ethical concerns, including the potential for algorithmic bias. AI systems must be designed to avoid perpetuating or amplifying existing inequalities. Regular audits and transparency in AI decision-making processes are necessary to ensure fairness and reduce the risk of discriminatory impacts on students.

4.2 Opportunities

With the fast development of AI technologies, the AI-enabled Metaverse has built a diverse ecosystem, from hardware devices to software algorithms. These advancements will benefit AI-enabled Metaverse applications for education in the future.

Emerging Metaverse Devices. Emerging Metaverse devices for education in recent years include a range of innovative technologies that are transforming the educational landscape. Devices like the Meta VR headsets, including the popular Quest 2, which underwent a permanent price reduction in 2024, making it more accessible for educational purposes. Interactive whiteboards and tables developed by Xunfei Illusion integrate XR and AI to create interactive teaching and learning experiences. Such devices allow students to interact with virtual objects in their actual environment, bridging the gap between theory and practical application.

The Popularization of Metaverse Applications. Driven by the increasing accessibility of technology and the growing demand for immersive experiences, has made AI-enabled Metaverse technologies in education more acceptable among educators and learners. By creating highly interactive and immersive environments, they enable learners to engage with content in a more intuitive and engaging way. This shift not only enhances the learning experience but also empowers educators with new tools to deliver content and assess student progress. Such innovations are not only making learning more fun and effective but also paving the way for a more inclusive and accessible education system where geographical boundaries are no longer a limitation.

Explosive Growth of Knowledge and Contents in Metaverse. The Metaverse, with its immersive and interactive nature, provides an unparalleled platform for learning. The development of multimodal processing and LLMs make generating teaching resources and contents more convenient. The explosion of knowledge and content within this virtual world offers educators and learners alike access to a vast and diverse array of educational resources. Through the Metaverse, students can engage in immersive learning experiences, exploring concepts and ideas in a three-dimensional, interactive environment. This not only enhances understanding and retention but also makes learning more engaging and enjoyable.

Smarter Recommendation and Discovery. The intelligent search engine in Metaverse systems utilize advanced algorithms to analyze vast amounts of data, including learning preferences, past performance, and areas of interest, to deliver personalized content recommendations. By matching educational resources with the unique needs and capabilities of each learner, these systems enable a more targeted and efficient approach to learning. For learners, this means no longer wasting time searching for relevant material or being overwhelmed by an excess of information. Instead, they are presented with resources that are tailored to their specific learning goals and abilities, thereby enhancing their learning experience and outcomes.

Boundarylessness and Sustainability. Firstly, the boundarylessness of the Metaverse provides endless possibilities for education. Students can access the Metaverse from anywhere, at any time, to engage in various educational activities. This boundarylessness not only gives more people the opportunity to receive quality education but also fosters the sharing and exchange of global educational resources. Secondly, the permanence of the Metaverse provides a solid guarantee for the preservation and inheritance of educational content. Educational content can be permanently preserved in digital form, impervious to the ravages of time. They can all be comprehensively recorded and displayed for future generations to learn from and reference. This permanence not only aids in the accumulation and transmission of knowledge but also offers abundant teaching resources for future education.

4.3   Paths to Better AI-Enabled Metaverse for Education

This requires multi-dimensional support from the perspectives of techniques, policies, and value. Generally, the technical level acts as the fundamental infrastructure that provides tools to solve exact educational problems. The policy level makes rules to guarantee the AI tools are appropriately executed obeying educational principles. The value level defines the goals and criteria, in terms of the education effect, to judge and guide the whole educational process, which is at the highest level.

Technical Level. *Advanced technology integration:* incorporate cutting-edge AI technologies, such as natural language processing and machine learning, to enhance the educational Metaverse's interactivity and intelligence. Integrate virtual assistants capable of understanding and responding to student inquiries in real-time. For example, the use of AI chatbots in online learning platforms has significantly improved student engagement and learning efficiency. *Data security and privacy:* ensure robust data protection measures are in place to protect student information and activity data within the educational Metaverse. Implement end-to-end encryption and regular security audits, as demonstrated by leading educational technology platforms that have successfully mitigated data breaches through rigorous security protocols.

Policy Level. *Regulatory frameworks:* establish clear guidelines and policies to regulate the content and activities within the educational Metaverse. Develop comprehensive policies that address issues such as copyright, student safety, and appropriate use of technology, as exemplified by the regulatory measures adopted by countries like South Korea, which have strict guidelines for online content and user protection. *Investment* *and incentives:* provide financial support and incentives to encourage innovation and development in the educational Metaverse. Introduce government-funded grants and tax incentives for companies and institutions developing AI-powered educational Metaverse solutions, similar to the initiatives undertaken by the European Union to promote technological innovation in education.

Value Level. *Enhancing educational quality:* utilize the educational Metaverse to deliver immersive and engaging learning experiences. Implement virtual reality (VR) simulations for science experiments and historical events, as illustrated by the successful integration of VR in medical and engineering education, which has significantly improved comprehension and retention rates. *Promoting inclusive education:* ensure that the educational Metaverse is accessible to learners from diverse backgrounds and abilities. Develop assistive technologies and accessible interfaces for students with disabilities, as demonstrated by the use of AI-powered screen readers and voice commands in online learning environments, enhancing educational opportunities for all.

5 Conclusion

The application of the Metaverse in the educational field has undergone a remarkable leap forward, thanks to the integration of AI. This transformation is attributed to five key characteristics. Firstly, the enhanced ability to tailor personalized teaching more precisely. Secondly, the provision of richer knowledge content. Thirdly, the convenient collaborative support it offers. Fourthly, the comprehensive and real-time teaching evaluation and analysis it provides. Lastly, its borderless nature. However, there are six major challenges in the implementation process. Firstly, the infrastructure for educational Metaverse is still inadequate. Secondly, ensuring privacy and security remains challenging. Thirdly, both teachers and students have limited experience and acceptance of the Metaverse. Fourthly, there are concerns regarding cost and sustainability. Fifthly, the potential negative effects of technology dependence could arise. Lastly, ethical issues and value biases in intelligently generated content need to be addressed. Through comprehensive optimization at the institutional, technological, and values levels, we can foster the development of a more advanced AI-enabled Metaverse, paving the way for a more perfect educational landscape.

Acknowledgments. This study was supported by the MOE (Ministry of Education in China) Liberal Arts and Social Sciences Foundation (No. 24YJC710008 and 23YJC710021) and the Research Project of Zhejiang Federation of Humanities and Social Sciences (No. 2025N010).

Disclosure of Interests. The authors have no competing interests to declare that are relevant to the content of this article.

References

1. Wang, H., et al.: A survey on the metaverse: the state-of-the-art, technologies, applications, and challenges. IEEE Internet Things J. **10**(16), 14671–14688 (2023)

2. Sami, H., et al.: The metaverse: survey, trends, novel pipeline ecosystem & future directions. IEEE Commun. Surv. Tutorials (2024)
3. Zhong, J., Zheng, Y.: Empowering future education: learning in the edu-metaverse. In: 2022 International Symposium on Educational Technology, pp. 292–295 (2022)
4. Wang, L., et al.: A survey on large language model based autonomous agents. Front. Comput. Sci. **18**(6), 186345 (2024)
5. Basyoni, L., Qadir, J.: AI generated content in the metaverse: risks and mitigation strategies. In: International Symposium on Networks, Computers and Communications, pp. 1–4 (2023)
6. Stanoevska-Slabeva, K.: Opportunities and challenges of metaverse for education: a literature review. In: Edulearn22 Proceedings, pp. 10401–10410 (2022)
7. Wu, Y., Zhang, K., Zhang, Y.: Digital twin networks: a survey. IEEE Internet Things J. **8**(18), 13789–13804 (2021)
8. Xie, Y., Gupta, J., Li, Y., Shekhar, S.: Transforming smart cities with spatial computing. In: 2018 IEEE International Smart Cities Conference, pp. 1–9 (2018)
9. Chang, L., et al.: 6G-enabled edge AI for metaverse: challenges, methods, and future research directions. J. Commun. Inf. Networks **7**(2), 107–121 (2022)
10. Fan, S., Yecies, B., Zhou, Z.I., Shen, J.: Challenges and opportunities for the Web 3.0 metaverse turn in education. IEEE Trans. Learn. Technol. **17**, 1989–2004 (2024)
11. Huynh-The, T., Pham, Q.V., Pham, X.Q., Nguyen, T.T., Han, Z., Kim, D.S.: Artificial intelligence for the metaverse: a survey. Eng. Appl. Artif. Intell. **117**(Part A), 105581 (2023)
12. Hwang, G.J., Chien, S.Y.: Definition, roles, and potential research issues of the metaverse in education: an artificial intelligence perspective. Comput. Educ. Artif. Intell. **3**, 100082 (2022)
13. Tlili, A., et al.: Is metaverse in education a blessing or a curse: a combined content and bibliometric analysis. Smart Learn. Environ. **9**(1), 1–31 (2022)
14. Gan, W., Qi, Z., Wu, J., Lin, J.C.W.: Large language models in education: vision and opportunities. In: 2023 IEEE International Conference on Big Data, pp. 4776–4785 (2023)
15. Lyu, H., Cheng, Y., Fu, Y., Yang, Y.: Exploring a LLM-based ubiquitous learning model for elementary and middle school teachers. In: 6th International Conference on Computer Science and Technologies in Education, pp. 171–174 (2024)
16. Büyüközkan, G., Mukul, E.: Metaverse-based education: literature review and a proposed framework. Interact. Learn. Environ. 1–29 (2024)
17. Chen, X., Zou, D., Xie, H., Wang, F.L.: Metaverse in education: contributors, cooperations, and research themes. IEEE Trans. Learn. Technol. **16**(6), 1111–1129 (2023)
18. Holmes, W., Tuomi, I.: State of the art and practice in AI in education. Eur. J. Educ. **57**(4), 542–570 (2022)
19. Ak, O., Şen Akbulut, M., Soydan, S., Yildirim, E.: Designing educational metaverses: a literature review to determine guidelines. Interact. Learn. Environ. 1–19 (2024)
20. Jeon, J., Lee, S.: Large language models in education: a focus on the complementary relationship between human teachers and ChatGPT. Educ. Inf. Technol. **28**(12), 15873–15892 (2023)
21. BenedettDörr, J., BeatrysRuizAylon. L.: A survey on the metaverse aspects and opportunities in education. In: 2023 International Conference on Intelligent Metaverse Technologies & Applications, pp. 1–8 (2023)
22. Lin, H., Wan, S., Gan, W., Chen, J., Chao, H.C.: Metaverse in education: vision, opportunities, and challenges. In: IEEE International Conference on Big Data, pp. 2857–2866 (2022)
23. Qiu, Y., Isusi-Fagoaga, R., García-Aracil, A.: Perceptions and use of metaverse in higher education: a descriptive study in China and Spain. Comput. Educ.: Artif. Intell. **5**, 100185 (2023)
24. Bobko, T., Corsette, M., Wang, M., Springer, E.: Exploring the possibilities of edu-metaverse: a new 3D ecosystem model for innovative learning. IEEE Trans. Learn. Technol. **17**, 1290–1301 (2024)

25. Ahuja, A.S., Polascik, B.W., Doddapaneni, D., Byrnes, E.S., Sridhar, J.: The digital metaverse: applications in artificial intelligence, medical education, and integrative health. Integr. Med. Res. **12**(1), 100917 (2023)
26. Singh, H., Miah, S.J.: Smart education literature: a theoretical analysis. Educ. Inf. Technol. **25**(4), 3299–3328 (2020)
27. Xu, W., Meng, J., Raja, S.K.S., Priya, M.P., Kiruthiga Devi, M.: Artificial intelligence in constructing personalized and accurate feedback systems for students. Int. J. Model. Simul. Sci. Comput., **14**(1), 2341001 (2023)

Research on the Application and Countermeasures of Metaverse Technology in Retail Service

Yulin Li and Liangbin Cheng[✉]

School of Marxism, Huazhong University of Science and Technology, Wuhan 430074, China
{d202081326,chengliangbin}@hust.edu.cn

Abstract. The application of metaverse technology in the retail is often seen in the form of digital human, virtual store, virtual experience, virtual production, digital collection, etc., integrating online and offline interactive or only serving the virtual world. The retail metaverse has been initially established in the beauty makeup, garment industry, home decoration and automobile retail. There are some unique problems in the retail metaverse, such as new economic risks, increasing technological costs and barriers to user acceptance. The reasons for these problems lie in the imperfection of legal rules, the immaturity of technology development and the lack of individual coping ability. We need to improve laws and regulations, support the digital transformation of the retail and provide responsible public management services at the government level, develop advanced technologies and adhere to technology for the good at the enterprise level, and enhance digital ability and rational resolution at the individual level.

Keywords: Metaverse · Retail · Application · Problem · Cause · Countermeasures

1 Introduction

The metaverse is generally considered to be a virtual world parallel to the physical world, while two worlds are connected, mapped and interacted with each other [1]. On the basis of searching dozens of definitions of metaverse, some scholars have summarized the common characteristics of metaverse: avatars as user representation, technology used for world representation (i.e., AR, VR, MR), synchronicity reflecting the real-time component, interactivity with objects, immersion and realism describing the closeness to reality and the ability to experience telepresence, support of social collaboration (i.e., interaction between users), and permanence outlining the continuance and persistence of the metaverse [2]. Metaverse is the comprehensive application of new IT technologies, including network and computing, management, virtual and real object connection, modeling and management technology, virtual and real space interaction technology [3]. Because metaverse digitizes users through electronic devices to provide immersive experience, users can have two or even multiple identities, and can freely shuttle between the physical world and the virtual world. In this sense, the metaverse will fundamentally

C. Xing et al. (Eds.): METAVERSE 2024, LNCS 15429, pp. 114–123, 2025.
https://doi.org/10.1007/978-3-031-76977-1_9

change the existing mode of value creation and market transactions, and become an important force driving economic and social development. Retail is one of the industries that will be strongly influenced by the metaverse. At the same time, retail is one of the industries that invests the most in the metaverse.

Retail is a terminal business activity that provides a product or service to an individual or group. Compared with other industries, the outstanding feature of the retail is that the transaction behavior is dispersed and large, and the market situation is complex. Second, the transaction content takes into account both goods and services, emphasizing consumption experience. Third, the transaction object is the end consumer, pay attention to sales means. In the 2020s, the development of data and information technology brought about a new retail model of "online + offline + logistics" [4]. According to the specific field of service, the retail can be divided into catering industry, garment industry, beauty makeup, home decoration, product sales and other industries. 2021 can be seen as the beginning of the retail metaverse.

The research status of retail metaverse. Compared with the traditional retail stage, the retail metaverse has the potential to bring consumers interaction, immersion, inspiration and satisfaction through new technologies. The virtual experience presented by the integration of advanced technologies can better meet people's needs of ability, autonomy and belonging [5]. The metaverse brings new competitive advantages to retailers by forecasting and formulating appropriate marketing strategies. The marketing strategy is to enhance virtual and real experience, customer focus and gamification [6]. Studies based on the resource-based view have found that the adoption of metaverse technology in retail has sustainable advantages in terms of eco-friendliness, user willingness to use and product innovation [7]. Chinese academics pay more attention to the digitalization of retail. The modern retail has gathered new momentum from digitalization, gained support from new ideas and technologies, and spawned new industries, new business forms and new business models [8]. A large number of studies have shown that digitalization accelerates the turnover rate of commercial capital in the retail process, reduces transaction costs and operating costs. Digitalization has a heterogeneous impact on regional and urban retail development [9].

In general, the existing research covers the composition technology, advantages and characteristics of the retail metaverse and specific application industries, etc., focusing on the characteristics and advantages compared with traditional retail. Relatively speaking, the existing research has not paid enough attention to the actual application status and effect feedback of the metaverse technology group, the possible threat of industry change, and the acceptance degree and adaptation attitude of specific people in the face of the metaverse retail. The following will explain the application, problems, the causes of the problems and the possible solutions of retail metaverse.

2   Application and Prospects of Retail Metaverse

2.1   Application of Retail Metaverse

The application mode of metaverse technology in the retail is mainly divided into two categories. The first category is the integration of online and offline, which serves the interaction of the virtual and physical world. There are several typical manifestations as follows. Digital human act as brand spokesmen and brand recommendation officers, and live virtual broadcasts all day to help the publicity and drainage the entity. Build a virtual store to deliver brand culture and design concepts while providing convenient services. Virtual experience to realize cross-time trial and convenient selection. In general, through real-time live broadcasting, interactive experience, intelligent logistics and digital settlement, it constitutes a seamless connection between online and offline.

The second category is only for the virtual world service. Virtual production, to meet personalized needs, design avant-garde, bold and novel. Users will be expected to "shop for virtual garment, pay for it, upload a full body photo or avatar, create a costume, show off the look" on the platform. Virtual collections, giving virtual value to real brands, creating digital assets in an all-round way, making digital production lines and digital collections, etc. NFT products to convey the brand aesthetic concept and it can aggregate IP content in the form of blind boxes and scenes.

2.2 Prospects of Retail Metaverse

Beauty Makeup. In the digital marketing process release virtual brand spokespeople, hold new product launch activities in the virtual space, launch creative makeup, and improve brand exposure. Elizabeth Arden, NARS and other beauty brands are launching immersive virtual stores, virtual makeup trials, personalized customization and other services. In the virtual store, users can not only learn the brand story and product knowledge, but also try on makeup using the virtual shapes provided by the brands, choose the right products according to their skin conditions, and participate in the development and production of beauty products.

Virtual Garment. 3D modeling technology realizes the fit sewing, and the physical simulation technology allows the fabric on the model showing natural folds and draping. The image rendering technology results in a detailed rendering of the garment. The garment in retail metaverse can reduce the labor, logistics and time costs, improve development efficiency, reduce resource waste, and achieve environmental protection goals. Virtual live broadcast, virtual runway show, fitting mirror, digital exhibition hall, etc., to gain user attention and enhance interactive experience. Digital avatars try on clothes and display matching for users to improve user experience satisfaction.

Home Decoration. Ikea launched the software and the virtual model room service. Users can use AR home placement function, take photos of real rooms, upload them to the design program, can realize intelligent identification of scene items and generate interactive 3D images with accurate dimensions and viewing angles, users can erase existing furniture from the virtual scene, place new IKEA furniture, to quickly change and evaluate design proposals. In the retail metaverse, home decoration uses digital twin technology in the design process. The construction process is simultaneously displayed by 3D virtual scenes. The inspection process is intelligently recognized by AI and tested by sensors.

Automotive Retail. Designers can design and test the appearance, structure and parts of the vehicle in the virtual space, which can quickly complete the design task and reduce the production and testing costs. They can simulate different use scenarios and conditions and conduct a more comprehensive evaluation of the safety performance of the vehicle. In the sales and marketing segment, retailers can hold various forms of automobile exhibitions and promotions to increase brand awareness and sales. In the metaverse, through a full-fidelity 3D car configurator, Users have a more comprehensive understanding of the vehicle, while reducing the cost and time of test driving (Fig. 1).

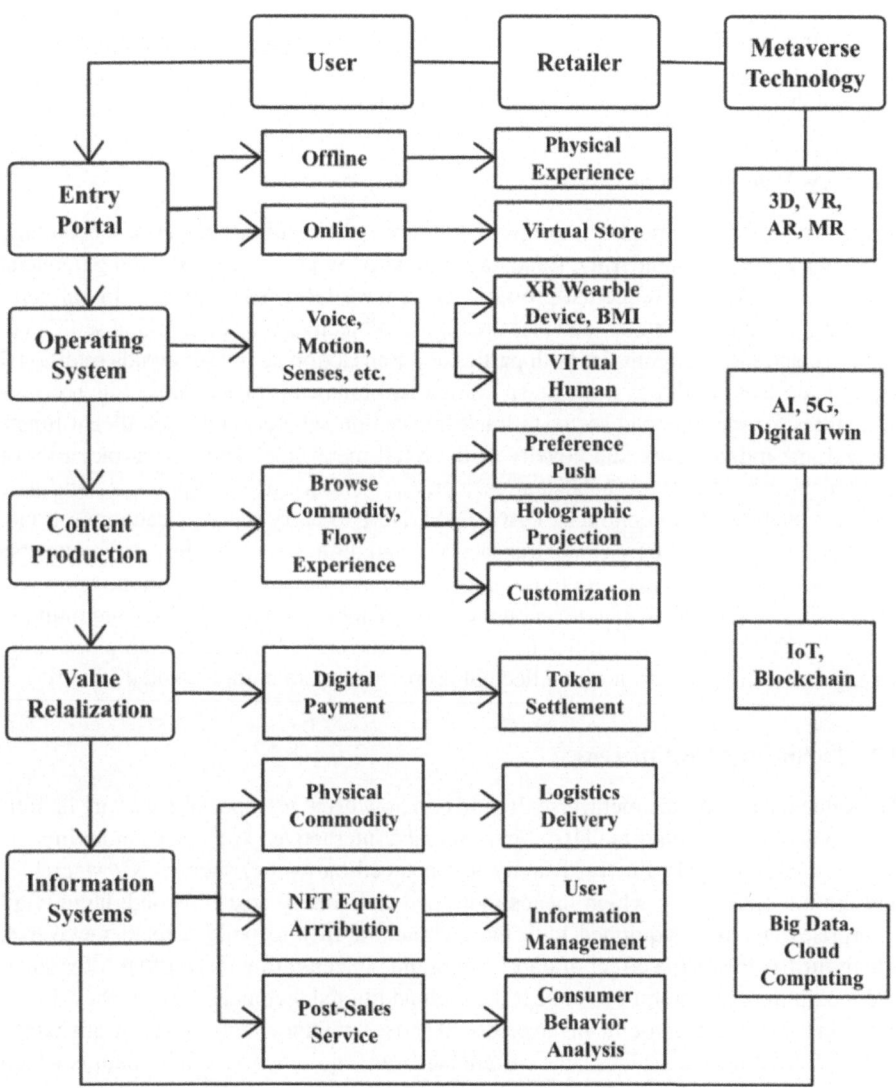

Fig. 1. A New Model for Retail Metaverse Service

3 Problems in the Retail Metaverse

The novelty of the retail metaverse format makes it easy to overlook the problems and risks that arise in its application. In fact, the combination of the metaverse technology and the characteristics of the retail may lead to some unique practical problems. First, the complex transaction situation in the retail metaverse poses challenges to enterprise operation and government management. Second, the transaction content attaches importance to the sense of experience, which needs the support of advanced technology. Third, the transaction object is for the public, and the acceptance degree of different groups is different. The problems are concentrated in the following aspects.

3.1 New Economic Risk

With the rapid development of the digital economy of the retail metaverse, new economic risks such as money laundering, fraud, tax avoidance and other acts disrupting financial order and infringing intellectual property rights have emerged. First, the digital commodities traded in the retail metaverse are highly subjective and adopt digital settlement methods, and the anonymity of both parties and transaction addresses avoids traditional supervision from both physical transportation and financial transactions, which brings difficulties for the financial sector to track transaction subjects and track illegal funds. Second, the individuality and novelty of the retail metaverse is easy to attract a lot of investment, but some criminals steal user privacy and use new technologies and new concepts such as smart contracts, DAO, DeFi, NFT to carry out new economic fraud. Third, digital commodities, digital transactions, and digital assets in the retail metaverse are prone to tax avoidance due to tax gaps in the absence of identification, rules, and supervision. Fourth, with a large amount of user generated content (UGC) and multiple freely circulating digital identities in the retail metaverse, the authentication, tracking, management and protection of intellectual property is more complex and difficult.

3.2 Technology Cost Increase

The value created by the metaverse depends on how users use special hardware or software to access the metaverse [10]. First, to make interactive experiences more immersive, companies need to invest heavily in advanced hardware, such as XR wearables and motion controllers, which means increased technology costs. Second, large retail enterprises are more equipped with the technical ability to build a retail metaverse, which further forms the effect of corporate brand concentration. It is difficult for small and medium-sized enterprises to bear the high additional technical costs. If they do not invest in the technology of the metaverse, enterprises will inevitably be at a disadvantage in the fierce competition. Third, the current hardware equipment is still immature, which often leads to virtual reality "hangover" and post-VR sadness [11]. If a user experiences eye strain, dizziness, nausea or limb discomfort while using a VR device, anxiety or intense feelings of sadness after exiting the VR device, it is difficult for them to fully engage and enjoy the virtual experience. To some extent, users seem to gain interactive experience from virtual space at the expense of physical and mental health, and bad use experience will bring technical pressure to users [12].

3.3   User Acceptance Barrier

On the one hand, the existence of digital divide objectively affects users' acceptance of the retail metaverse. In the process of global digitalization, different countries, regions, industries, enterprises and community groups, due to the economic development status, the understanding of information network knowledge, the application of digital technology and personal knowledge ability, age and other differences, will cause significant information gap and wealth disparity. Research shows that women, the elderly, people with low wages, people with less digital access, and people with low digital well-being reported significantly lower digital confidence [13]. The retail metaverse will further divide those who benefit from digital technology and those who do not. On the other hand, when users enter the retail metaverse, they are easily induced to irrational consumption. The marketing advantage of the retail metaverse is to predict that by using big data and AI algorithms to accurately push information. Research shows that young users may over purchase NFT digital collections for novelty, and such conspicuous consumption often worsens rather than increases consumer well-being [14].

4   Causes of Problems in the Retail Metaverse

The problems in the retail metaverse are a combination of legal, technical, and personal issues. Partly because of the imperfection of legal regulations and social norms, the rapid development of new technologies leads to gaps in the definition and punishment of related problems. Partly of the problem is immature technology, to be further research and innovation. Partly because of the users lack of self-control and it is easy to be induced to overconsumption.

4.1   Incomplete Laws and Social Norms

First, in the retail metaverse, it is not clear that hackers steal goods, services and intellectual property, user information leakage, network fraud, financial crimes, the definition of false information and the supervision and punishment of criminal behaviors. Second, the value definition and evaluation mechanism of the metaverse virtual products have not been established systematically. Ownership of virtual goods is not universal across multiple metaverses. Rules regarding the authentication of value, ownership, and reproduction rights of personal digital collections need to be developed and regulated. Enterprises produce digital products for profit, and such NFT digital collections can bring good return on investment in the short term due to the artificially designed scarcity. Third, laws on data security and privacy protection are not yet complete. Whether the retailer's request for personal information authorization is compliant, and whether the retailer's rights and responsibilities for the use and collection of personal information are compliant are not clearly delineated in the legal level. Fourth, how to guarantee the digital vulnerable groups to enjoy the services provided by the retail universe is also a practical problem. The retail metaverse is still a key area to be covered and maintained by laws, regulations and social norms.

4.2 Immature Technology Development

First, technology immaturity is the root cause of the current technology cost increase. The rapid change of new and old technologies and high manufacturing costs have led to high equipment prices. For example, PICO not only launched three generations of VR headsets in one year, but also reduced the price by 37.5% to 62.5%. Second, immature technology leads to management loopholes. Management schemes cannot cover frequently changing technologies in a timely and effective manner, resulting in new economic risks, political regulatory risks, and information protection risks associated with the application of new technologies, such as NFT fraud, political commodity trading and privacy disclosure. Third, immaturity of technology affects user experience. User-friendly technologies should be designed to be simple and easy to operate. Wearing heavy external devices can easily lead to virtual reality sequelae such as 3D vertigo, and complex device usage thresholds artificially reinforce the digital divide. The immature development of digital twin technology and virtual reality technology leads to the distortion of digital reality.

4.3 Insufficient Personal Capacity

First, the construction of digital infrastructure affects individuals' digital learning ability and adaptability, and the social equity and inclusive value of digital resources are based on objective social and economic conditions. Second, the curiosity of the retail metaverse to meet the interest of experience, the attraction of personalized customization and the comparative pressure from peers can easily make users, especially teenagers, lost in it. Virtual products have the importance of providing social emotional value. Users tend to spend too much time in the retail metaverse when purchasing virtual goods and obtaining emotional value such as identity and group belonging. Third, the emotions generated by users in the immersive experience are real, and the consumption impulse will produce real consumption behavior. Irrational consumption will often occur, which may lead to resource waste and excessive consumption. Fourth, the anonymity of the virtual world may encourage some people with low moral quality to do uncivilized behavior, and because the behavior in the virtual world is digital, it is easy to reduce people's sensitivity to immoral and unfriendly content.

5   Countermeasures

The government, enterprises and individuals (users) should join forces to build a "responsible metaverse" and adhere to the construction of a humanized retail metaverse field of sustainability, convenience and shared well-being. The government should focus on standardizing the development environment of the retail metaverse, enterprises should focus on overcoming technical problems in the retail metaverse, and individuals should focus on improving their coping ability and using the retail metaverse to better serve themselves.

5.1   At the Government Level

Theoretical Suggestion. First, the government should speed up the improvement of the relevant laws and regulations of the retail metaverse. The European and China had set laws and regulations provide the basic framework for the application of metaverse data. It is necessary to speed up the construction of legal content such as privacy protection and data security, platform fair competition, digital asset protection, patent protection act and algorithm discrimination review, improve laws and regulations related to digital economy governance, and build a data network security system. Second, it is important to support the digital transformation of the retail. The government is actively building a digital transformation service platform to provide consulting services, program design and technical support for enterprises in their transformation. The government should encourage enterprises to complete digital transformation by providing incentives such as tax breaks and revenue incentives to enterprises. Third, the government should provide responsible public management services. There are still many difficulties in managing the virtual world, and the government is trying to find the right scale between laissez-faire and strict regulation. It is great for bridge the digital divide as far as possible by educating the society, promote social equity in digital resources.

Practical Experience. Experience in legal system development and international cooperation is available. For minors among vulnerable groups, China has formulated the Law on the Protection of Minors, the Regulations on the Protection of Minors and the Opinions on Strengthening the Protection of Minors, providing a "technology + ethics + law" paradigm for the legal governance of the metaverse. At the international level, governments of many countries have promoted international cooperation in the governance of retail crime, and the current cooperation between Interpol (ICPO), the Financial Action Task Force and international organizations such as G20, G7 and APEC has achieved good results in the handling of cross-border telecom fraud cases.

5.2   At the Enterprise Level

Theoretical Suggestion. First, Enterprises should strengthen the research and development of metaverse related technologies. By developing holographic projection technology that can fully display goods, and tactile technology that can experience the texture and temperature of goods, enterprises will bring users a more realistic virtual reality experience. Enterprises further develop the 3D modeling technology and resolution requirements to enhance the simulation degree of virtual reality, and realize the virtual to the real, the virtual to promote the real, the virtual to strengthen the real. Second, enterprises should strengthen research and development of technologies related to data security and privacy protection. Enterprises should design and apply machine learning algorithm models with both efficiency and fair value, use a variety of technologies such as user information anonymity protection, information watermarking, and information traceability, and enhance blockchain transparency and self-build VPN system encrypted transmission and other ways to integrate user data security and privacy protection throughout the entire technical process of information collection, transmission, application and storage. Third, enterprises should develop differentiated strategic positioning to cope with the impact of virtual retail on physical retail.

Practical Experience. There is retail reform experience for enterprises' reference. Cloudpick applies the metaverse technology to offline physical stores, changing the underlying logic of the "flow economy" of the traditional retail pursuit of small profits and quick sales, focusing on the differentiated needs of individuals and the value of the whole life cycle, and mining the "single customer economy". In 2023, Cloudpick cooperate with LAWSON to launch intelligent non-inductive payment stores. In the Web 3.0, this method protects user privacy, respects user data autonomy, pointing out a new path for the retail industry to create the ultimate consumer experience.

5.3 At the Personal Level

Theoretical Suggestion. First, individuals should take the initiative to learn digital technology skills. Scientific cognition of the operation mechanism of the retail metaverse help users understand how to obtain services, how to reduce the risk and put themselves in a beneficial role. Second, individuals should improve their capacity for autonomous control and self-regulation. Users should clearly define the boundary between virtual and real, and find ways to realize their personal value in the physical world to resist technology addiction. Third, individuals should be sensible in identifying new forms of consumerism. Individuals should have a clear understanding and positioning of their own consumption power, consume according to their real needs, and walk out of the trap of precision marketing. Finally, individuals should increase the vigilance of their own privacy protection, carefully consider the necessity of data authorization to the platform, and develop a good habit of clearing the digital records used by devices. Users should also be more sensitive to distinguish infringements, cultivate a sense of proactive rights protection, and be alert to exploitation, oppression and inequality caused by "digital biological and chemical weapons".

Practical Experience. In July 2022, the world's first "Metaverse Arbitration Court" was built in Guangzhou, and in November, it accepted the "Metaverse Arbitration Case", that is, the offline commercial infringement case of metaverse digital collections. The AI "Xiaozhong Yun" of the Metaverse Arbitration Court received more than 1,000 inquiries in just three months. This path sets a model for individual rights protection in the retail metaverse.

6 Conclusions

Retail is a mass oriented, large number of transactions, emphasizing the experience of goods and services in the field, we hope that the retail metaverse can combine the characteristics of the retail to play the technical advantages of the metaverse, so that everyone can enjoy the quality services provided by the retail with the blessing of the metaverse technology. At the same time, the imperfection of the current metaverse technology determines that its combination with the retail will face some unique problems, such as new economic risks, increased technical costs and user acceptance barriers. There are legal, technical and personal issues in the retail metaverse. Governments, enterprises, and individuals work together to explore solutions to the problems from multiple levels, so as to promote the development of the retail metaverse in the direction of mutual benefit and mutual sharing.

Acknowledgment. This research was supported by the National Social Science Foundation General Project, "Research on the political attribute of science and technology and its policy significance under the background of the new scientific and technological revolution" (No. 23BZZ094).

References

1. Dionisio, J., Burns, G., Gilbert, R.: 3D virtual worlds and the metaverse: current status and future possibilities. ACM Comput. Surv. **45**(3), 1–38 (2013)
2. Lee, U., Kim, H.: UTAUT in metaverse: an "Ifland" case. J. Theor. Appl. Electron. Commer. Res. **17**(2), 613–635 (2022)
3. Wang, W., Zhou, F., Wan, Y., et al.: A survey of metaverse technology. Chinese J. Eng. **44**(4), 744–756 (2022)
4. He, R.: Analysis on the evolution and development path of digital retail industry under the global marketing environment. J. Commercial Econ. **14**, 23–27 (2021)
5. Caboni, F., Pizzichini, L.: Smart extended reality in the metaverse-tailing: the rise of new retail landscape. In: Geroimenko, V. (ed.) Augmented Reality and Artificial Intelligence. Springer Series on Cultural Computing, pp.307–321. Springer, Cham (2023). https://doi.org/10.1007/978-3-031-27166-3_17
6. Bruni, R., Colamatteo, A., Mladenović, D.: How the metaverse influences marketing and competitive advantage of retailers: predictions and key marketing research priorities. Electron. Commer. Res. **24**(2), 965–982 (2023)
7. Abumalloh, R.A., Nilashi, M., Ooi, K.B., et al.: The adoption of metaverse in the retail industry and its impact on sustainable competitive advantage: moderating impact of sustainability commitment. Ann. Oper. Res. (2023)
8. Shi, Z.: Research digital economy enabling the high-quality development of the retail industry: connotation, characteristics and strategies. China Circ. Econ. **04**, 4–7 (2024)
9. Qiu, J., Feng, S.: The heterogeneous impact of digital economy on the development of regional, urban and rural retail industry in China. Mercantile Theory **15**, 5–9 (2022)
10. Hennig, T., Aliman, D. N., Herting, A.M., et al.: Social interactions in the metaverse: Framework, initial evidence, and research roadmap. J. Acad. Market. Sci. (2022)
11. Benjamins, R., Rubio Viñuela, Y., Alonso, C.: Social and ethical challenges of the metaverse. AI Ethics **3**, 689–697 (2023)
12. Issa, H., Dakroub, R., Lakkis, H., et al.: Techno-eustress and techno-distress: a metaverse investigation. Inf. Resour. Manag. J. **35**(1), 1–21 (2022)
13. Bentley, S.V., Naughtin, C.K., McGrath, M.J., et al.: The digital divide in action: how experiences of digital technology shape future relationships with artificial intelligence. AI Ethics (2024)
14. Dittmar, H., Bond, R., Hurst, M., et al.: The relationship between materialism and personal well-being: a metaanalysis. J. Pers. Soc. Psychol. **107**(5), 879–924 (2014)

Audiobooks in the Cultural Metaverse: Reimagining New Quality Productive Forces and the Future of the Audio Culture Industry

Xinyi Lin[✉] and Nengqing Tao

Communication University of China, Beijing 100024, China
xinyilin@cuc.edu.cn

Abstract. The integration of AI technology in audiobook creation and publishing has introduced significant changes and challenges within the audio arts field, demanding a reevaluation of traditional concepts and models. This paper analyzes the implications of AI-driven audiobook publishing through the lens of new quality productive forces and the cultural metaverse. It deconstructs the "textual poaching" logic of generative AI within the audiobook sector, employing a Marxist methodological approach to assess how these technologies reshape the cultural industry. The study highlights four dimensions—new forms of productive forces, new production factors, new production relations, and new production efficiency—revealing that contemporary audiobook publishing exhibits distinct production dynamics compared to the past. The fusion of data by generative AI, the "de-originalization" of cultural materials, human-machine co-creation models, and the structural transformation of traditional cultural industries present expanded and innovative opportunities for China's audiobook sector. By incorporating the cultural metaverse perspective, the paper explores how immersive and interactive elements of the metaverse further influence the creation and consumption of audiobooks, offering new insights into the evolution of this cultural sector.

Keywords: new quality productive forces · generative AI · audiobook publishing · cultural metaverse · cultural industry · intellectual property rights

In 2024, the emergence of generative AI has facilitated the visual representation of science and art. It is projected that by 2026, the rapid growth of the generative AI market will reach $6.5 billion. It can be said that generative AI is increasing in importance and application across various industries, including media and entertainment. This is not only evident in its ability to enhance user search experiences based on massive datasets but also in its capacity to autonomously create cultural content such as text, audio, and video. However, there are concerns about the risks associated with the content generated by AI, such as privacy issues, biases, and intellectual property rights. Recently, artists collectively sued AI companies like Stability AI, Midjourney, and the art website DeviantArt, claiming that generative AI uses artists' works to train image generation models without authorization, akin to an "art heist." Despite this, generative AI continues to impact the publishing processes in areas such as imagery, audio, writing, and marketing. On March

C. Xing et al. (Eds.): METAVERSE 2024, LNCS 15429, pp. 124–133, 2025.
https://doi.org/10.1007/978-3-031-76977-1_10

16, 2023, the United States Copyright Office (USCO) issued a statement recognizing that automatically generated works by AI are not protected under copyright law.

As a part of the cultural industry, the application of AI in audiobook publishing, through technologies such as automated text-to-speech conversion and voice cloning, not only alters the production process but also redefines the boundaries of creation and trade. The emerging AIGC (Artificial Intelligence Generated Content) paradigm acts as a powerful driving force, providing unprecedented strategic opportunities for accelerating the development of new forms of productive forces in the audio-visual industry. Currently, China's audiobook publishing industry is characterized by the rise of technical voices, the establishment of new listening models, and an increase in industry share. However, it faces challenges related to copyright protection, content value, industry operations, and editorial professional competence. Generative AI liberates the production capabilities of audiobook publishing and becomes a ubiquitous technological tool, but existing practices in China's audiobook industry are insufficient to address the dilemmas brought about by AIGC, including intellectual property, ethical considerations in creation, and aesthetic values, as well as the impact of new technologies on the concept of artistic originality. Today, global audiobook publishing and emerging streaming media industries compete fiercely over licensing rights and attention economies, resulting in increasingly conservative market strategies and aesthetic choices.

The problem addressed in this article arises from these considerations: what changes will works created through human-machine co-creation or with minimal human involvement bring to the audiobook publishing industry? How should we view the content of audiobooks formed through "textual poaching" and human-machine co-creation? In the face of evolving knowledge production methods, is it necessary to update our concept of originality and critically reshape the landscape of the cultural industry in the context of technological innovation? If we shift our perspective from an uncertain future to the history of media and theory, can we activate and understand a different kind of artistic originality and essence as a solid foundation for responding to technological and cultural transformations? The impact and challenges that AI technology poses to today's audio arts should be seen as an opportunity to reconstruct the audio arts and challenge the hegemony of the global cultural industry centered around them. By leveraging the advantages of previous development stages, we can form new concepts for the AI production and dissemination of audiobooks within a more complex ecosystem of content production and distribution.

1 Theoretical Framework

1.1 New Forms of Productive Forces

New forms of productive forces are characterized by innovation taking a leading role, breaking away from traditional economic growth models and productivity development paths. They are marked by high technology, high efficiency, and high quality, aligning with the principles of new development. Fundamentally, they concern the transformation of past development into economic outcomes. Since President Xi Jinping first introduced the concept of new forms of productive forces during a meeting to promote comprehensive revitalization in Northeast China, many scholars have conducted extensive research from various perspectives. They have analyzed the essential features of new forms of productive forces and discussed their internal logic, mechanisms of action, and specific implementation paths from the perspectives of Chinese-style modernization, high-quality regional development, digital economy, and new development concepts.

1.2   Marxist Theory of Cultural Industry

Based on the ideas of Theodor Adorno and Max Horkheimer, Marxist critical theory of the cultural industry emerged. In their book Dialectic of Enlightenment, they write that in capitalist societies, cultural products are industrially produced and consumed, losing their critical spirit and independence, becoming tools to maintain the capitalist system. The cultural industry leads to the standardization and commodification of culture, where the uniqueness and revolutionary nature of art are replaced by homogenized entertainment demands—a phenomenon still evident in today's media and entertainment industries. We observe that artworks and other cultural products increasingly conform to commercial logic rather than their own artistic value or expression.

Within the Marxist framework, the development of productive forces drives changes in production relations, which in turn affect broader social structural changes. From a Marxist perspective, the application of generative AI technology in audiobook publishing not only challenges traditional modes of audio content production but also breaks the cultural standardization criticized by Adorno and Horkheimer—AI technology can produce personalized and diverse cultural products at scale and low cost. This near-revolutionary improvement in cultural production efficiency is as powerful as the introduction of the Spinning Jenny. However, the balance between technology and art remains a continuous competition, and AI may lead to new forms of cultural homogenization. Algorithms often optimize output based on user data and historical consumption patterns, potentially reinforcing existing cultural consumption patterns and preferences.

Thus, this paper constructs a theoretical perspective that integrates new forms of productive forces with the cultural industry, analyzing the new state of the cultural industry triggered by AI in audiobook publishing. Based on critiques of traditional cultural industry theories, we explore AI audiobook publishing and the cultural industry from the perspective of new forms of productive forces.

2   Understanding AI Audio Publishing Through the Lens of "Textual Poaching"

2.1   What is "Textual Poaching"?

In the era of internet culture, the concept of "textual poaching" provides us with an important cultural theory foundation and a media historical perspective for understanding issues of "artistic appropriation" in the age of intelligent technology. Therefore, the charge of "artistic appropriation" faced by AIGC (AI-generated content) is familiar. Jenkins describes this "poetics of poaching" as the active participation and innovation in culture through the recombination and rearrangement of popular culture elements, involving the contest over "text ownership and the interpretation of meaning." Michel de Certeau, in his postmodern critique, views cultural consumers as "poachers," who "steal" mainstream cultural products in their daily lives and imbue them with new meanings. De Certeau advocates for the creation of an active reading subject, one that should navigate between texts like a nomad, "poaching" on others' literary "territories" to appropriate content that is useful or pleasurable, highlighting the proactivity of reading and the dissolution of authorial authority.

Focusing on the framework of "textual poaching," we gain insight into how generative AI creates audio art content through imitation and recombination of existing artistic elements. This imitation is not mere plagiarism but rather similar to cultural poachers seeking inspiration and materials in the jungle of texts, rearranging and endowing them with new life and meaning. Some practitioners with an optimistic view see this as a digital inheritance and recreation of existing "artistic legacies."

2.2 The Technical Logic of AI Audio Publishing

AIGC has been widely applied in areas such as image recognition, image segmentation, object detection, and image generation, assisting in character modeling, scene reconstruction, and the simulation of physical effects in computer vision technology. In discussions about generative AI films, scholars have pointed out that works created through the deep learning of a director's style or through the learning of massive amounts of data, blending the achievements and styles of multiple artists, pose significant challenges to copyright attribution for AI films.

Similarly, generative AI audiobooks face a similar situation–algorithms extending into the audiobook publishing industry, such as AI-assisted scriptwriting, algorithmically generated audiobook audio, or the use of natural language processing and sentiment analysis to analyze scripts, assist in scriptwriting, or automate the creative process. Himalaya's proprietary speech synthesis technology has achieved the "reproduction of the voice of Shantian Fang," while the AI writing assistant Caiyun Xiaomeng can complete the creative production and intelligent writing of web literature. The popularity of AI "Sun Yanzi" fully demonstrates the availability, malleability, and accessibility of smart soundscapes. Nevertheless, discussions regarding the technological originality of AI publishing continue to be raised in intellectual property cases – in the Stable Diffusion case, the artist's lawsuit argued that "every output image is entirely derived from copies of copyrighted images. For these reasons, every mixed image must necessarily be a derivative work," suggesting that anything created by AIGC cannot be original, viewing it as essentially a "21st-century collage tool." In reality, AIGC technology does more than replicate and recombine its training data; it understands and learns the patterns, structures, and relationships within the data through deep learning mechanisms, creating novel and original outcomes beyond mere replication of training data. For example, in writing or painting, it can create new plots, characters, or images not present in the training data. AIGC typically uses unsupervised learning, which means there are no specific, predetermined goals during training, relying instead on self-learning and generation for innovation. This iterative process allows AI to understand and create complex artistic works far beyond simple "collage" skills. For instance, the artificial intelligence music composition platform AIVA (Artificial Intelligence Virtual Artist) can create structurally complex musical works. AIVA masters the patterns and structures of music through deep learning, generating original music that goes beyond simple combinations of notes, encompassing melodies, harmonies, and rhythms. With the support of AI voice synthesis and sound editing software, the content ecosystem of audio media will experience a comprehensive expansion.

2.3 Intellectual Property Controversies Surrounding AI Content

The human-AI collaboration model (HAI-C) enables generative AI, after absorbing a vast array of existing artistic elements and styles, to create new, original works. However, this challenges the foundations of modern intellectual property. The Stable Diffusion litigation reflects the art world's general attitude toward AI creation, with discussions primarily revolving around the legal framework of intellectual property, viewing AI as a new form of utilizing intellectual property. However, simply attributing these issues to AI technology and treating them as entirely new problems is clearly unjust. Before AI became a "challenger" in artistic creation, mimicking specific artists' styles or blending various artistic styles had already appeared in multiple creative fields, such as Quentin Tarantino incorporating different film texts and references into his unique "style." In 2022, the Netflix documentary "The Andy Warhol Diaries" featured AI company Resemble AI "deep faking" Andy Warhol's voice to read his own diaries.

Developed by OpenAI, ChatGPT is a dialogue language model based on natural language processing (NLP) and is among the most advanced language models currently available, playing a role in the text publication of AI-generated audio content. Additionally, AIGC technologies often use generative models like Generative Adversarial Networks (GANs) or Variational Autoencoders (VAEs), which generate novel samples that are similar to but not identical to the training data, significantly reducing direct human involvement. The ChatGPT model developed by OpenAI, also based on NLP technology and using the Transformer network structure, can generate contextually relevant responses based on user input, predict subsequent words and sentences, and even create complete articles and poems. These are examples of AIGC applications based on deep learning.

While this understanding may temporarily resolve some intellectual property disputes and labor conflicts, as intellectual property expert Andrés Guadamuz points out, AI autonomous agents that rely on programmers or human guidance are still understood and incorporated into the current intellectual property system under traditional frameworks of ownership, responsibility, and obligation. Moreover, AI systems represented by neural networks have the potential to produce works with minimal human involvement. This compels us to confront the core challenge that AIGC technologies pose to the human knowledge production system, including original ideas. Guadamuz mentions that these AI systems, represented by neural networks, are based on deep learning technology, emulating the structure and function of the human brain's neural networks, and rely on big data-driven autonomous learning and training, enabling computers to achieve performance equal to or exceeding that of humans in specific tasks. At the same time, generative models commonly used in AIGC, such as GANs or VAEs, can generate new samples that are similar but not identical to the training data, greatly reducing human participation and achieving almost fully automated work creation.

From cultural fusion to data fusion, new media technologies are fundamentally updating and iterating traditional methods of knowledge production and dissemination. As mentioned earlier, artificial intelligence technology has been widely applied in the cultural industry, not limited to automated applications in daily life such as smart maps and photo beautification. "In a sense, artificial intelligence is now ubiquitous." However, once AI technology solves a problem in a particular field and is put into practical application, it is no longer seen as exclusive to that field. In terms of intellectual property, the contradiction faced by AI technology lies in the fact that, despite AIGC applications not being limited to specific professional domains or industrial processes, but stemming from fundamental changes in knowledge production methods, they have had a widespread impact across all knowledge and creative fields. Indeed, AI is already changing every aspect of our daily lives in ways that are more profound and extensive than we anticipated (Table 1).

Table 1. The Primary Media Forms and Cultural Flows Characteristic of Different Stages of Civilization

Civilization	Media	Cultural Flow	Senses	Sensory Coordination
Primitive	Oral	Traditions and customs inherited through oral communication	Audio	Highly depend on hearing and oral communication Strong interpersonal links
Agricultural	Paper	Information can be widely spread through books and newspapers	Visual	Emphasis on visual sense and reading ability Encouragement on individualism and linear thinking
Industrial	Electrical Wave	Information can be spread much more faster than before through broadcast and television	Audio and Visual	Equal emphasis on hearing and visual Promoting collectivism and globalization

(continued)

Table 1. (*continued*)

Civilization	Media	Cultural Flow	Senses	Sensory Coordination
Digital	Internet	Information communication is instant and multidirectional	Audio, Visual and Tactile	Combination of multi-sensory Interactive and diverse
Metaverse	Metaverse	Immersive and augmented experience of reality	Audio, Visual, Tactile, Olfactory and Taste	All-sensory experience Fusion of virtual and real world

3 Critical Analysis of the Audio Publishing Cultural Industry in the Era of Generative AI

3.1 New Productive Forces: Data Fusion in Generative AI

Generative AI has brought about unavoidable changes to the audio publishing industry, and opposing these changes would be akin to opposing "the automobile, airplane, or internet." Marshall McLuhan once noted that railways did not merely introduce motion, transport, wheels, or roads; rather, they accelerated the scope of human activities, expanded human functions, and created new types of cities, professions, and leisure forms. Therefore, compared to its diverse applications in the cultural industry, the impact of generative AI on "changing the scale, speed, and mode of human activities" is clear and profound: new knowledge and creativity emerge from "data fusion," the creation of new knowledge using data from different sources. This provides a new perspective for understanding and evaluating the role of AIGC (Artificial Intelligence Generated Content) in knowledge production. Jenkins' concept of "convergence culture" posits that the convergence of digital technology and internet culture environments leads to participatory cultures and the emergence of collective intelligence, allowing people to influence shared experiences through individual or collective choices. This is not just the integration of technologies or merging of media platforms but a process of cultural transformation, the formation of new social, cultural, and political forces, and the reshaping of relationships between technology, industry, market, community, and audience. The framework of smart media technologies represented by AIGC continues this cross-disciplinary, cross-cultural, and cross-medium collective innovation behavior. In the process of data fusion, all creators and works participate in AIGC creation in some way, forming a more radical and larger-scale model of collective creation.

3.2 New Production Factors: The "De-originalization" of Cultural Materials

Text is the carrier of thought. Deep thinking, aesthetic perception, and artistic creativity have long been considered unique human abilities. However, these applications can automatically identify features and patterns from large datasets without manual feature selection or design, enabling independent learning across multiple domains and reducing dependence on humans. Through AI scriptwriting or automatic language generation applications, the knowledge production model based on language – considered the last bastion of innovation – now faces ongoing challenges. The 2013 science fiction film "Her" tells the story of a man falling in love with an AI, which exists only as a voice in his ear. It could be said that generated voices can still evoke emotions. Just as novels and comics had their unique cultural and aesthetic values before the development of electronic information technology, the link between audio art and humans remains inseparable and ever-present.

In traditional humanism, acquiring knowledge typically relies on rational thought and observation of the world. However, the introduction of AIGC technology has led to a de-subjectivization of the creative process. Through deep learning and other techniques, machines can understand human artistic creation and create new works of art, transforming these creative generation tools from mere tools to systems sharing subjectivity with creators. For example, users of the Dramatron system question the identity of the co-author in human-machine co-created texts, pondering whether it should be seen as a writing tool or a collaborative creation system. This relationship of subjectivity between humans and machines gradually forms in such questioning and triggers deeper discussions about the concept of originality and post-human experiences with minimal human involvement.

3.3 New Production Relationships: Human-Machine Co-creation in AI Audio Publishing

In the traditional theoretical framework of the cultural industry, participatory technologies and collective cultural production and dissemination have deconstructed the identity of artists as independent copyright holders and renegotiated power dynamics in a "media production shaping competition" model. The use of AIGC may fundamentally liberate artistic creation from a person-centered author model, making it a product of human-machine collaboration. This cooperative approach directly challenges the core of modern property rights concepts, particularly regarding the authority and subjectivity of individual creation in traditional humanism.

In the field of AI audio publishing, this human-machine co-creation model further reinforces the role of human subjectivity. Currently, three main AI voice technologies have been applied: (1) voice conversion, involving the transfer of one character's voice characteristics, such as Obama's timbre and intonation, to another character, like Trump, while maintaining the original speech content, used in scenarios such as celebrity impersonation, voice acting, and voice alteration; (2) voice cloning, focusing on training specific voice models, such as Zhao Zhongxiang, to read new text information aloud, applied in simultaneous interpretation, smart assistants, voice synthesis, and audiobooks; (3) general text-to-speech, which uses pre-trained voice models to convert text information into speech, used in advertisements, promotional videos, audiobooks, and video dubbing. Traditionally, the production of audio publications heavily relied on the creativity and skills of individual artists or voice actors, who imbued works with unique artistic souls through their vocal expressions and understanding of the text. When using generative AI for content publication, such as replicating the distinctive voice of a figure like Shan Tian-fang, data training, monitoring, artistic guidance, and style control must be conducted within a human-machine cooperation system, along with the innovative integration of technology and art. In this process, the role of humans has not been weakened but rather actively participates and influences the application and development of technology. Even as discussions around responsible AI theory and industry voices increase, they do not diminish the human subject's participation in the publication of audio content. As we observe over time, the consumption of novels is not affected by product substitution; people can enjoy multiple novel works simultaneously without reading one preventing them from reading another. Similarly, the disappearance of jobs depends on society's demand for corresponding products or services, not the intervention of AI technology. Although new technologies like AI can improve efficiency, the value and demand in fields like literary creation in audio publishing are not solely determined by production efficiency. That is, whether traditional manual labor or modern intelligent production, positions exist only if they meet societal needs. Therefore, some scholars argue that AI should bear certain responsibilities, but essentially, various generative AIs currently can only display statistically derived human information, reflecting human morality visible in data. AI cannot yet function as an independent moral agent.

3.4   New Production Efficiency: Structural Upgrading of Traditional Cultural Industries

The continuous impact of new technologies on the paradigmatic cultural industries and existing industrial orders has always existed. Adorno and Horkheimer believed that in the capitalist system, cultural products have become commodities produced primarily for profit maximization, not for artistic expression or creative freedom. This commodification leads to the standardization and homogenization of cultural products, as market forces tend to promote widely popular and easily marketable content. We can see today that global film cultural industries, such as the franchise model established by Disney and the big data and algorithm recommendation strategies of streaming media companies like Netflix, are shaping a competitive media ecosystem. As traditional film giants like Disney, Warner, and HBO enter the streaming media market, they bring the franchise production model into this highly competitive field, gradually transforming the global streaming media industry into a continuation of the traditional film industry's competitive logic, leading to an "information flow world war" over data resources and property rights. In this war, the innovation and aesthetic value of film art become increasingly marginalized. Audio publishing, as part of the "listening" aspect of streaming media audiovisual content, holds a significant share of the market and cannot escape this context. This guides our attention beyond the immediate legal and ethical challenges to observe the more critical and revolutionary cultural potential of new technologies. If we view this open platform as a tool driven by digital production and dissemination technologies, we find that this model emphasizes appropriation and collaboration, values positive feedback and construction for participants' works, and contrasts sharply with the competitive nature and individualistic authorship model of commercial publishing and media production. AIGC applications challenge the concept of authoritative cultural production, making it possible for non-professional artists to create works of art.

This structural upgrading of production efficiency driven by technological advances is a phenomenon worth observing in the current development of AI.

Classical historical materialism affirms that the development of productive forces and technology liberates human potential. Humans have always had a desire to share what they see, hear, touch, and feel with others. One could say that the fusion of technology and art paves the way for this desire. From oral history, printing, television broadcasting, the internet, to virtual reality technology, these advancements continuously expand the boundaries of human sensory extension and immersion. Therefore, artificially distinguishing AI as either an automated efficient tool or an intelligent creative subject and treating them differently is dangerous and potentially fatal, leading to a "contemporary" dilemma when dealing with AIGC issues. We must avoid trivializing new media technologies represented by AIGC, viewing them as simple tools for creative realization, and also avoid mystifying and alienating them, ignoring their real impacts.

References

1. Lv, Z.: Generative artificial intelligence in the metaverse era. Cognitive Robot. **3**, 208–217 (2023)
2. Chen, C., Fu, J., Lyu, L.: A pathway towards responsible AI generated content. arXiv preprint arXiv:2303.01325 (2023)
3. van der Zant, T., Kouw, M., Schomaker, L.: Generative Artificial Intelligence. Springer, Heidelberg (2013)
4. Abbott, R.: Artificial Intelligence and Intellectual Property: An Introduction, Research Handbook on Intellectual Property and Artificial Intelligence, edited by Ryan Abbott. Edward Elgar Publishing, P. 9 (2022)
5. Guadamuz, A.: Do androids dream of electric copyright? Comparative analysis of originality in artificial intelligence generated works. Intellect. Property Q. (2017)
6. Manovich, L.: AI Aesthetics, p. 7 Strelka Press (2018)
7. Jenkins, H., Ito, M., Boyd, D.: Participatory Culture in a Networked Era: A Conversation on Youth, Learning, Commerce, and Politics, p.181. Polity Press (2015)
8. Jenkins, H.: Art happens not in isolation, but in community: the collective literacies of media fandom. Cult. Sci. J. **11**(1), 8 (2019)
9. Adorno, T.: Dialectic of Enlightenment. Verso Books (2016)
10. Manovich, L.: The Language of New Media, p. 289. MIT Press, Cambridge (2002)
11. Jenkins, H.: Textual Poachers: Television Fans and Participatory Culture, p. 23. 2nd ed., Routledge, Milton Park (2015)
12. Jenkins, H.: Convergence Culture: Where Old and New Media Collide, p. 408. New York University Press (2020)

Author Index